Acknowledgments

While preparing this work for publication I was helped by many people and particularly by the following: Felix Cronin, Michael Cronin, Fr Gearóid O'Sullivan, Liam M. Collins, Laurette Kiernan, Margot Gearty, Michael Magee, Eileen O'Donovan, Sheila Donovan, Fr F. J. Gilfellan, Ralph Sutton, Dan Bryan, W. J. Comerford, W. J. O'Brien, Catherine Donohoe, Dermot and Maire Coghlan, Kevin Boland, Alan Eager, Dan Nolan, J. J. Kenrick, G. A. Meagher, Seán Collins-Powell, Fergal Tobin, Hilda Allan and my wife Cáit. To all of them, and to the Department of Defence and the National Library of Ireland, many thanks.

León Ó Broin

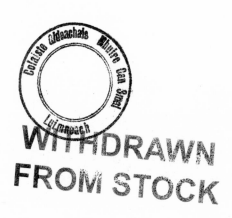

IN GREAT HASTE

The Letters of Michael Collins and Kitty Kiernan

In Great Haste

THE LETTERS
OF MICHAEL COLLINS AND
KITTY KIERNAN

Edited by León Ó Broin

GILL AND MACMILLAN

First published 1983 by
Gill and Macmillan Ltd
Goldenbridge
Dublin 8
with associated companies in
Auckland, Dallas, Delhi, Hong Kong,
Johannesburg, Lagos, London, Manzini,
Melbourne, Nairobi, New York, Singapore,
Tokyo, Washington

7171 1287 X

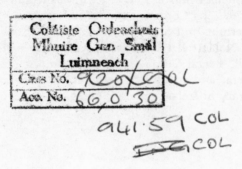
Origination by Galaxy Reproductions Ltd, Dublin
Printed in Great Britain by
Biddles Ltd, Guildford and King's Lynn

In Great Haste

Central to this correspondence — indeed at the very heart of it — is a young lady who lived with her brother and sisters in the Greville Arms, a modest family hotel in the main street of the North Longford market town of Granard, Co. Longford. She shared with them the running of the hotel, for which she had got some little training, and the adjacent store which embraced a grocery, a hardware, timber and undertaking business, as well as a bar. Around the corner, on the other side of Market Street, was another part of the establishment, a bakery which supplied bread to the town and much of the neighbouring countryside. The young lady was Catherine Brigid, or more usually Kit or Kitty, Kiernan. She shared good looks, charm and grace with her sisters, one of whom, Christine or Chrys, was more seriously disposed than the others. Indeed, as our story opens, Christine was said to wear a perpetually worried look. She had reason to be worried. The two eldest children in the family, twin girls, had died in their teens between 1907 and 1909, and in 1908 — their parents, Bridget and Peter Kiernan, had also died within a couple of months of each other. A relative, Andrew Cusack, who was a draper in the town and himself the father of six boys and a girl, was to be the family guardian but he, too, died within a very short time. Chrys, the eldest of the surviving children, was not yet 19, Kitty 16, Helen Josephine 15, and Maud 14. Larry was 17, but being the only boy, he was brought home from St Mel's, the diocesan college where he had been a boarder, to become effectively the head of the family concern. It was probably

1

assumed that the girls sooner or later would marry and leave the homestead.

There was always plenty of work to be done about the place; in the hotel, which had its own bar, of course, but mainly in the store, or shop as they called it. There was an entrance to the store from the main street, and another from the yard at the back where there was plenty of stabling for horses. Carts coming in from the country would be left there, while their owners did their leisurely shopping in the store, moving from one mahogany counter to another. Having paid their bills or extended their credit, they could, if they felt like it, have hot drinks and sandwiches served to them through a hatch from the hotel kitchen, or find something more stimulating at the bar. There there were a couple of snugs to which the women folk, in the fashion of the time, could resort for a glass of port.

The place hummed with activity, especially on Monday, the market day. The girls shared out the jobs as they came nearest to hand but Maud, who was recognised as 'the practical one', had a little office to herself at the back of the shop where she looked after the accounts. She also kept a wary eye on what was going on in the bakery. Larry came more and more into the picture as time went by. Like his father before him he had a real flair for business and took advantage of the improved lot of the farming community during the Great War, and the valuable passing trade. The North had not yet been cut off from the rest of Ireland politically: commercial travellers came regularly to Granard from Belfast to join those from the South, and Lough Gowna, which was only a few miles away, attracted holiday-makers. There was a good deal of movement northwards, too, from which the hotel benefited. Enniskillen, Belfast, Bangor and Portrush are frequently mentioned in Kitty's letters.

They were a highly respected family, and Larry, or Laurence Dawson Kiernan to give him his full name, was to win considerable popularity. He was elected to the chairmanship of the local district council and held the position for twenty-five years. He was a keen sportsman, played a good game of tennis, travelled to coursing matches, bred

2

and showed hunters at the Dublin Horse Show, and rode with the Longford Harriers. He loved to hunt and, whenever it was Granard's turn to be the centre for a day, the huntsmen, among them military officers stationed in the county, would find their way sooner or later to the Greville Arms. His formal education, interrupted by the death of his parents, was not resumed but his sisters did not suffer in that respect. They did not go back to the Loreto in Bray, Co. Wicklow, however, where they had been boarders, but to Pearse's experimental school, St Ita's, in Dublin, where one of their teachers was Louise Gavan Duffy, the youngest daughter of the Young Irelander of that name. Andrew Cusack was responsible for the decision to send the girls to such a school, along with his own daughter Minah. An advanced nationalist, he shared Pearse's educational ideas, but what the girls remembered of St Ita's, as compared with Loreto, was that there was less formal classwork to be done, that they were taken on visits to the city's museum and art galleries, and that classes were held sometimes in the school garden when the weather was clement. In any event, without absorbing anything overtly nationalist such as a knowledge of Irish and of Irish history, the school appears to have been a pleasant prelude to an adult life to which they brought money, imagination and talent. They were naturally welcome at every social event, and held parties of their own in the long flower garden behind the hotel, and 'musical evenings' in the drawing room on the first floor of the hotel. There their capacity to entertain was abundantly evident. They could even provide from among themselves a small instrumental group; and they could sing. Kitty had not a particularly good voice but she knew what a song demanded, and one piece from her repertoire reflected what was to become a personal problem for her — 'I know where I'm goin' but the dear knows who I'll marry', for there was no shortage of suitors. Her letters suggest that within little more than a year as many as five young men were interested in her.

The Kiernan girls had personality and position as well as a dress sense which was widely recognised. In this regard they had the advantage of what might be called a resident couturier.

3

This was Paul Cusack, one of their guardian's sons and a somewhat legendary figure. He, unsuited to any occupation Granard had to offer, had been to India as tutor to a Maharajah and, on his return, while waiting for something else to turn up, applied his artistic talent to designing clothes for his cousins.

The political changes that followed the Rising of 1916 affected the Kiernan family in a significant way. The hostilities did not extend to the County Longford, of course, but Alec McCabe, an IRB organiser from Sligo, put up in the Greville Arms on Easter Sunday night and from there he attempted to organise an assault on the enemy's communications, their railway lines and telegraph wires (*Irish Times*, 1 May 1970). The Kiernans knew nothing of this; McCabe was just a transient guest. In May of the following year, things were different. A Longford man they might have known, Joseph McGuinness, who was in prison for his connexion with the Rising, was nominated to oppose the Irish Party's representative in a by-election in the south of the county. He succeeded in winning the seat, if by the slenderest of majorities — 39 votes on a recount — an effective slogan in the campaign being 'put him in to get him out'. In the crowd that came into Longford town one evening to help in the election Brighid Lyons Thornton, a relative of McGuinness, saw a handsome young man and recognised him by his accent, his chuckle, and the twinkle in his eye. This was Michael Collins: 'You'd know him the minute he was in a place'. All the accommodation was already filled, but 'we had found this lovely hotel in Granard, which was run by four beautiful sisters and their brother, and we decided to put Michael there. They were lovely, glamourous girls, and had all the right ideas.' They were also keen business girls, and mature beyond their years. (*Curious Journey*, 108).

So Michael went to Granard with, possibly, Harry Boland and Gearóid O'Sullivan, and would have met, there or on the way, another Paul Cusack who had been with them in the internment camp in Frongoch in North Wales and was now sharing their zealous promotion of the national movement. In Granard Collins may have been attracted first to Helen

4

Kiernan, who 'oozed charm', but she was probably already involved elsewhere, so Michael turned his attention to Kitty. He was soon to acquire a reputation in the area. In April 1918 he was arrested and lodged in Sligo Jail for having at Legga, near Granard, made a speech that was calculated to cause disaffection. He was formally charged in Longford and given bail to appear at the next assize, but didn't. Having appeared in Granard, where he was given a royal welcome in a street lined with Volunteers, he travelled to Dublin and went on the run. From this time onwards Longford was linked in his mind with his native Cork.

Collins and Boland jointly held a unique position in both the political and military wings of the movement. They were members of the Supreme Council of the clandestine Irish Republican Brotherhood (IRB) and used the authority this gave them to place men of their choosing on the governing bodies of Sinn Féin and of the Irish Volunteers, which later became the Irish Republican Army (IRA). Collins was the spearhead of the fight (Tom Barry in *Curious Journey*, 169). Through being the General Headquarters Director of Intelligence in the Volunteers and Dáil Minister of Finance, he accomplished great things as the struggle with the British developed into a physical War of Independence. Boland, also a tremendous worker, was to be associated closely with de Valera in the campaign in the United States in 1919 and 1920 for the recognition of the Irish Republic. In the British general election, held at the end of 1918, Collins and Boland both became members of parliament, Collins for Cork South, and Boland for Roscommon. But at the first meeting in January 1919 of Dáil Éireann, which the election enabled to be created, they were recorded as being absent. They were, in fact, in England engineering the escape from Lincoln Jail of de Valera and Milroy who were being held for their connection with an alleged German Plot to stage a second insurrection.

The Letters
A couple of disjointed pages from a letter Collins wrote to Kitty Kiernan suggest that this may have been done under cover of an alleged conference. The escape occurred on the

night of 3 February 1919, and Collins and Boland went thereafter to London. Collins was back in Dublin exactly a week later (Collins to Austin Stack, 10 Feb. 1919), but he returned to England for some reason and came back to Ireland openly on 6 March with the general body of the German Plot prisoners who had been released that day under a general amnesty.

Letter 1

Mícheál, Valentia Island, to Kitty, Monday evening, no date, but probably February or March 1919.

My darling Kitty,

You must have been imagining all kinds of queer things about me for my prolonged silence, but I had a very busy time in London and our stay there was much longer than we expected — only got home on Friday night last and strange thing I again travelled with the first of the released prisoners — Larry Ginnell[1] and Willie Cosgrave![2] I am sure ye are all excitement and delight at the prospect of Paul's return. How I wish I could be there. In London we had a very difficult job to get accommodation and, on the night of our arrival there, I had to be content with sleeping on a mattress placed on the floor. Altogether we had a decidedly Bohemian outing, but we had to combine a good deal of business with the maximum of pleasure. One night I had a slight attack of poisoning. . . .

III

. . . Is it not a strange coincidence that I should be travelling with the first batch of prisoners again? I scanned all faces on board carefully hoping that Paul[3] would be amongst them, because nobody seemed to know who was or was not released at that time. I do hope he is none the worse for his confinement.

My time in London was quite a whirlwind rush. Our conference lasted eight days — sitting from 10 a.m. to 5 p.m. and every evening we were booked up with friends for theatres, concerts, and even dances. On only one night did we have a proper rest. We stayed in the Regent Palace Hotel after the first few days — just fancy there were fifteen hundred people staying there, and they were a very interesting study. Many times in this hotel we had to line up in queues for seats for meals!

1. Laurence Ginnell (1854-1923), the Nationalist MP for Co. Westmeath who resigned his seat in 1917 and joined Sinn Féin.
2. A common enough pronunciation at that time of (W. T.) Cosgrave.
3. Paul Cusack.

The 'darling' in that letter was, I think, used rather casually. It would be mid-summer of 1921 before Collins would speak to Kitty in the terms of deep affection which the word can imply. Harry Boland's more lively concern at this time for the same Kitty and the assumption that she would follow his movements with interest are implicit in a telegram announcing an arrival time, and in a postcard, written in the early months of the American campaign.

Harry, Cincinnati, Ohio, to Kitty, 9 October 1919.

Dear Kitty,
    A card from Ohio in rememberance. I am off with the Chief on the great tour, and I will send you a card as I go along. We are having great meetings and wonderful success. I often think of you, and your happy family, and the pleasant times I had with you. I suppose ye will all have forgotten me by now. Anyway keep a warm corner for me in that gay heart of yours. My regards to Maud, Chrys and 'the Parisian Rose' [Helen], not forgetting Larry, Mr and Mrs Paul Cusack, and all friends. I will pay you a visit early next year D.V., and I will give you all the story.
                         Slán is Beannacht. H.B.

    By this time Collins had successfully organised an issue of Republican Bonds; some Volunteers in Tipperary, without authority, had captured and killed a couple of policemen, and shot two more in rescuing a prisoner; the Royal Irish Constabulary, which was an armed force nearly 10,000 strong, fortified their barracks through the country, and these the Volunteers proceeded to attack. Dáil Éireann was formally outlawed as 'a dangerous organisation', and Collins set up an extensive intelligence network inside and outside the British state organisation in Ireland, making use of a select 'Squad' of men to eliminate informers and other persons considered undesirable.

Boland was home on leave from the States in June 1920 as the process of attack and counter-attack, of suppression and retaliation continued. Policemen were shot on sight; raids on private houses were made by British forces on a vast scale; internment camps were opened; towns shot up and curfews imposed. The Lord Mayors of Cork and Limerick, who had connexions with the Irish Volunteers, were assassinated in their homes; and 'Auxiliaries' and 'Black and Tans' put in an appearance to support the RIC who, in many villages and towns, were under pressure to abandon their barracks.

It is clear from the next incomplete letter from Boland that his smouldering affection for Kitty, whom he had met again, had been rekindled, and that he intended, if possible, to marry her. The reference in the letter to Father Michael O'Flanagan, the Vice President of Sinn Féin, suggests that Kitty, through the hotel connexion or otherwise, knew the Roscommon priest.

Letter 2

Harry Boland, Dublin, to Kitty Kiernan, 17 June 1920.

My dear Kitty,

I must grab a few minutes from a very busy day to write a line to you. As Paul[1] will have told you, I am hungry to see you again ere I go on the great hike.

You will think it very strange of me no doubt, seeing that I have just returned, yet I am sure you will understand why it is that I return again to 'Granard's Ancient Moat'.

I have just left Fr O'Flanagan[2], having spent the last few hours with him. I need not say how truly wonderful my few days holiday were to me. I feel, however, that I treated you

8

rather unfairly in keeping you from your slumbers. Do say that you are now recovered. If I could only be with you I would indeed try to make you happy. It may be that I will come back soon again from overseas. Please God it may be our lot to win the fight so long waged for freedom. If so, we can all feel proud of our generation. 'Tis but in vain for soldiers to complain'. Yet I long to be in Ireland, more so than ever that I have hopes to win the girl I love best in all the world. . . .

Excuse this disjointed note. I am writing it in a tobacco store with crowds all round. With fondest love,

Yours ever,

H.

1. Paul Cusack.
2. Father Michael O'Flanagan.

———————————

On 26 June he sent her a 'goodbye and best love' telegram from Southampton as he faced back to the United States.

Things went from bad to worse in the second half of 1920. Creameries, mills and bacon factories were destroyed. The sacking of towns continued, and individuals, many of them unconnected with the IRA, were murdered in cold blood. Terence MacSwiney, the Lord Mayor of Cork, who represented mid-Cork in the Dáil, was found with illegal documents on his person, refused to recognise a military court, and died after a prodigious hunger strike. Kevin Barry, a university student of 18 years, was captured, after an ambush in which six soldiers died, and was hanged. Collins, aware that a company of British intelligence agents were out to destroy his organisation, had the houses they resided in Dublin entered and practically all of them wiped out in their beds. That was Bloody Sunday, 21 November 1920, a day made bloodier still by the nature of the reprisal. A large crowd watching a football match in Croke Park was fired on: twelve men and women shot dead, sixty wounded, and some hundreds injured in a stampede.

The Volunteers had begun to organise some full-time active service units or flying columns. That formed in Longford in November 1920 was led by Seán MacEoin, a blacksmith whose forge was in Ballinalee, and who was known personally to the Kiernans. Collins had come down from Dublin in September to confirm MacEoin as Director of Operations for Co. Longford and parts of Leitrim and Cavan. In the following month the Longford Brigade Council decided to 'remove' the local District Inspector of the Royal Irish Constabulary, a young man from Macroom named Philip St John Howlett Kelleher, who had been staying on and off in the Greville Arms. He was said to have insulted women during a raid on a house in Ballinalee, and to have declared that he had been sent to Longford to spill blood and intended to do so. But when Samuel McCoy of the American Committee for Relief in Ireland questioned locals on the subject they had little to say against Kelleher; what was hated was the fact that he was in command of an enemy force (*Roscommon Herald*, 4 March 1922). In any event the decision to kill him was ratified by GHQ, but was made conditional on the death of Terence MacSwiney or Kevin Barry. MacSwiney died on 25 October, and Barry was hanged on 1 November.

Knowing that the Kiernans were sympathetic to them — Larry, at risk to himself, had enabled a collaborator from the British side to be smuggled out of the country — the Volunteers wanted to avoid shooting Kelleher on the hotel premises. Larry was, therefore, asked to explain to the D.I. that, in view of the general boycotting of the police that was being enforced, it would be in his interest to cease coming there, but this Larry declined to do. It would detrimentally affect the hotel's business, he said, and bring him openly into conflict with the British establishment. As an alternative, Kelleher's visits were closely observed, and it being noticed that he customarily left the hotel every night at eleven to visit the barracks, a night was chosen on which he was to be shot as he came out on to the street. On the appointed night, 31 October, he had not appeared by 11.30, and the two Volunteers waiting for him, hearing a piano being played in an upper room and assuming that a party of some sort was in progress, went into the hotel bar and found Kelleher drinking at the counter with members of the North Longford Sinn Féin executive and a priest, and fired at him.

In McCoy's dramatic report, 'Kelleher put down his half-finished glass limply, and fell dead before the spilled liquid could drip to the floor'. The priest gave him the last rites.

The rest of the company scattered and fled in sheer terror, leaving Larry Kiernan and his sisters 'to carry the can'. They were arrested and brought to the military barracks in Longford but released the next day with the exception of Kitty who appears to have been detained somewhat longer. Meanwhile a Constable Cooney who had gone in mufti to the Ballinalee area, where MacEoin had his headquarters, to reconnoitre the situation was fired on and fatally wounded. Towards midnight on 3 November eleven lorries of military entered Granard, sacked the town, and burned down the hotel. The Kiernans, anticipating that this was likely to happen, took out of the building what they could; and what the girls took was believed to reflect their dominant personal interests. Chrys took all the religious objects she could find and a spool of thread; Kitty took the silver; Helen the dresses; and Maud the account books. Later, if a customer claimed that she owed nothing, Maud would produce the relevant book from under a counter and say, 'Ah, but I'm afraid you do.'

Collins, apparently unhappy about how the affair had been handled, brought Seán MacEoin to Dublin for questioning, and wrote to Kitty. His letter is not in the collection, but Kitty's reply, which is, indicates its contents. We can only guess at the means by which their letters were exchanged, and why Kitty had been specially singled out by the British military. The interest Collins and Boland had been showing in her may have had something to do with it.

The hotel was rebuilt out of compensation money, but it was well into 1922 before it could be lived in again. In the rebuilding, little attempt was apparently made to modernise it. Water had still to be carried to the rooms, and the chamber pots emptied by hand. While the rebuilding was going on, the family lived for a period in Omard House before taking a large flat over a shop on the New Road, just at the back gate of the hotel.

Letter 3

Kitty Kiernan, Granard, to Michael Collins, 20 January 1921.

My dear

Very many thanks for your kind letter. Please forgive me for not replying sooner, but we have been very busy trying to get things fixed up. We are carrying on business, but have made no definite arrangements until we have peace. I had quite an experience when I was arrested, but I must say the military were very kind to me, and I felt well, considering.

With all good wishes for the coming year, and I hope you will say a prayer for me.

Yours sincerely,
Kitty Kiernan.

Kitty kept a letter from a friend which recalled the troubled times through which she had passed.

L. F. Daly, Inniscarrig House [Western Road] Cork — to Kitty, 24 December 1920.

My dear Kitty,

You will be surprised to hear from an old friend, but as both Cork and Granard have been suffering for their Country I cannot leave the opportunity pass without dropping you a line to condole with you in your terrible experience recently. How are you getting along all these years? And your sisters, are they still alive and well? A number of the boys that used to visit Portrush have got married. . . . I knew that poor young fellow Kelleher that was shot, quite well. He used to play a lot of Rugby football and would possibly have got his Irish Rugby Cap this season. You must have had a terrible time during that terrible night. We had an appalling time here, shots up and down the streets both day and night. I was held up and searched frequently, in fact so often that we used to walk up to the Black and Tans to be examined again. I saw by the paper that you were released after 3 days. It was only yesterday I saw the cutting in the newspaper. Frank Bradley and other boys are A.1. and send their regards.

I was in Dublin recently and heard you were there, but did not know where.

Drop a line some day. With best wishes for the festive season and hoping you have quite recovered.

Very sincerely yours,
L. F. Daly.

De Valera and Boland returned to Ireland in that month of December, and from his Dublin home, Harry sent Kitty a short note. Whether he was aware at that moment of the details of what had happened in Granard we do not know. His letter would suggest that he thought that conditions in North Longford were more or less normal, which, of course, they were not.

Letter 4

Harry, the Crescent [i.e. 15 Marino Crescent, Clontarf] to Kitty, 16 January 1921.

My dear Kitty,

I'm off to Paris on to-morrow night to attend the Race Convention.[1] I hope to return within ten days and I will then, D.V., come to Granard and renew old 'friendships'.

Tell Larry I will be delighted to join him in a hunt and, for your own information, I don't care if I never return from the hunt.

Love to all,
Harry.

1. A Congress of the Irish Race (Fine Gael) was held ultimately in Paris in January 1922.

The national struggle continued during the first half of 1921, its principal features being the systematic exploitation by the Irish flying columns of the tactics of ambush, the development of guerilla war *à l'outrance*, while a still more intensive form of retaliation was being meditated by the British government (*Ireland since the Famine*, 412). Then, before this happened, hostilities stopped. Seán MacEoin was a prisoner and awaiting execution, despite desperate efforts to rescue him, but his life was ultimately saved by a truce, beginning on 11 July 1921, whose purpose was to enable a political Anglo-Irish settlement to be explored.

13

Collins and Boland, emerging from the shadows, were now in a position to renew 'friendships' with the Kiernans in Dublin and Granard. They visited their British-designed parliamentary constituencies; a general election in May had been held to give effect to the Government of Ireland Act, intended to establish separate parliaments in Northern and Southern Ireland. In the election Collins was returned for Armagh as well as Cork and went to see his constituents there with Boland, who had also been to his Roscommon constituency in the company of the Irish-American F. J. Walsh. Subsequently, Boland and Joseph McGrath carried one of the letters that were being exchanged between de Valera, acting for the Dáil cabinet, and the British Prime Minister, to Gairloch in Scotland where Lloyd George was holidaying.

Letter 5

Micheál, Gresham Hotel, Dublin to Kitty, 2 August 1921.

My dear Kitty,

Got back all right. When I was speaking to you I had a kind of idea that the Horse Show[1] was coming off this week, but of course it's next week, and that's a very long time to wait to see you. I must continue that talk with you. At the moment I don't know if I'll be able to go down for the coming week-end, but I'll try. The only thing is that I must come back on Sunday evening. When do you come up yourself? I mean what day, and what time? Am really anxious to see you.

Kindest regards
M.

1. The annual show organised by the Royal Dublin Society at Ballsbridge, Dublin.

That the 'friendships' had ripened to the point that Collins was definitely in competition with Boland for Kitty's affection is evident from the following three letters. We have not Kitty's 'nice note'.

14

Letter 6

Mícheál, Gresham Hotel, Dublin, to Kitty, 21 August 1921.

My dear Kit,

Many thanks for your nice note received yesterday morning. Did you get my letter (or rather scrap) written here early on Friday morning?

Harry is back here this morning. Will that entice you to come to town, to give you that chance to which he is entitled? Do you remember what I said to you about this?

I cannot write just now as I am laughing too much at Harry who yarns about things across the Atlantic.

No doubt you'll see some of the boys to-day and perhaps you'll send back some messages. Yet I suppose they may not get as far as Granard as the day is bad and, owing to the arrival, they started late.

Have you started to forget yet? I hope not.

Yours with love,
M.

Letter 7

Mícheál, Dublin, to Kitty, 22 August 1921 on a page from a loose leaf pocket book.

My dear Kit,

I have just got your rebuke or, first, your salutation. But why the rebuke? I wrote yesterday and I wrote on Thursday morning or Friday morning. Why, then, are you *absolutely* out with me? Perhaps because I did not travel [to Granard] yesterday, but I had to work, and I am writing this under great difficulties at a Dáil meeting, but I must write to avoid *a* misunderstanding. The accompanying Letter[1] was not posted last night as it was too late. Also I had no stamps.

Hope you are not too tired to-day.

Love,
M.

1. That of 21 August (Letter 6).

Letter 8

Mícheál, Wicklow Hotel, Dublin, to Kitty, 31 August 1921.

My dear Kitty,

This isn't a letter either — there is no need to emphasise it. How are you now — and since? All my arrangements were shattered again last night, or rather this morning. I had to talk very very high politics from 10.30 until 2.30, and high politics are very tiresome unless one is in very good form. Then to bed, as old Pepys would say, thinking of the previous night when, as I explained to Harry, I stayed up most of the night advocating his claims[1] — isn't that rather nice?

You asked me to write. This is writing, but not a letter. I go to Armagh on Sunday. Are you betting that the Ulster Specials[2] will have a pot at me?

Love,
M.

1. Collins may have been referring to the discussion, within the Supreme Council of the IRB, of the line Boland had taken in the United States in the conflict between de Valera and the Clan na Gael leaders Daniel Cohalan and John Devoy.
2. The Royal Ulster Constabulary was supported by the Ulster Special Constabulary which had been formed in 1920 out of the Ulster Volunteer Force which had been revived in that year as an additional form of defence against the IRA.

The Dáil had met in private session on the morning of 22 August in the Mansion House, Dublin, primarily to consider peace negotiations with the British. There was a full attendance of deputies, including Seán MacEoin, and the discussion lasted five days.

Collins was involved at two distinct levels during these days. With the discussions within the Dáil cabinet on the issue of peace, and in the IRB, of which he was now president and where concern was being expressed at the severance of the Supreme Council from the American Clan na Gael, led by Devoy and Cohalan, through, it was said, Boland having exceeded his instructions.

Collins takes up the story of the visit to Armagh. He chides Kitty about being introspective, a tendency of which we shall hear more later. His reaction to seeing the head of Blessed Oliver is to be noticed, as well as the order of persons he prays for as he lights a candle at the shrine. He assumes that Kitty had read the newpaper accounts of his visit. She probably has, and Harry Boland tells her more about it.

Letter 9

Mícheál, Dublin, to Kitty, 6 September 1921.

My dear Kit,
    Your letter was waiting for me yesterday on my return. I had rushed all day to get back in early afternoon — we left Clones at 7 in the morning — and I was very disappointed. However, I suppose I must put up with it. It really was not fair though. Please do not emphasise that point about your real self. I know what you say is right, and that is really all that matters, isn't it?
    We had a very busy time during Sunday and up to about 12 o'clock yesterday. Then we started for home, and had rather an interrupted journey! And no wonder, but we ended up well and had no trouble after Drogheda. In Drogheda I saw the head of Blessed Oliver Plunkett. It's simply marvellous, and also I lit candles there — the first for you and so on.
    Now goodbye. I do hope very very much that you will have a good jolly time and do come back to Dublin before you return home, and come back when I am here, not when I'm away. What did you think of Armagh?
Goodbye. With love,
Ml.

Letter 10

Harry, 15 Marino Crescent, Clontarf, to Kitty, 8 September 1921.

My dear Kitty,
    Sorry I missed you and M on Saturday. As a matter of fact we did not leave Dublin until Sunday morning for Armagh, where we had a very strenuous day. I have just gotten back

from Roscommon, having motored down with Frank P. Walsh. Everything passed off O.K. and I am truly happy to have the 'official' visit over and done with. This morning's papers seem to fancy or imagine that the British Cabinet have decided to invite *An Dáil* to send its men to Inverness on Sept. 20th. It may very well be that I shall be in Scotland during the negotiations, and I would very much like to see you ere we go. If, however, you are enjoying a very nice holiday in Donegal, I shall not ask you to break it, and will wait patiently for a later day. I have not seen 'the Doc' as yet, and will make it my duty to see him this week.

Michael and party had a very fine meeting at Armagh. We called at Clones, Co. Monaghan on our way home and spent a very enjoyable evening with O'Duffy[1] and Company. We arrived in Dublin on Monday evening at 5 p.m., having motored all the way. I left Dublin on Tuesday morning for Roscommon, and arrived back in town on Wednesday midnight. Some traveller! I do hope you will enjoy a complete rest among the hills of Donegal. If you a see a wee bit of white heather, you might pluck it for me and sent it for luck on my Scotch trip.

I have not and will not say a word to M. All things considered, you are the Doctor!

With fond love from
Harry Boland.

1. Eoin O'Duffy (1892-1944), Deputy Chief of Staff of the IRA, Commissioner of the Garda Siochana, Leader of Fine Gael, the National Guard and National Corporate Party. Organised an Irish Brigade to fight for Franco in the Spanish Civil War.

Letter 11

Harry, 15 Marino Crescent, Clontarf, to Kitty, 20 September 1921.

A Chuisle mo chroidhe,

If I had gotten the telegrams (you so kindly forwarded to me) ere I left Granard I would not now be here writing to you; rather would I be with you in your own dear home and so 'double cross' Collins and O'Sullivan who despatched the

wires for me. Seems to me that I have a hard road to travel
ere I can call you my very own!

Arrived in town and met 'the bunch' in the Gresham.
Gearóid had booked a box for the Gaiety and invited me
along, so I went and enjoyed the show OK. We had a nice
supper in the Gresham after the Theatre. 'Mopsy', Helen,
Gearóid, 'Nuck' Duggan and Mrs, Seán Ó Muirthuile[1] and
your humble. Meantime many of my pals (?) overtly asked
'How did you (meaning me) get on at Granard?' To all of
which I failed to respond. The telegrams were sent in the
hope that I would still be at Granard, and there was joy in
the camp when I arrived!

I am writing this short note to you ere I go to bed to say
how much I enjoyed my trip to see you and to say how
lonely I feel to-night. Even during the gayest moments of the
evening I was all the time thinking of you, Sweetheart, and
am certain you and I will be for all time lovers.

Needless to say I have not as yet reported for duty. I called
up the Chief on my arrival and he, very kindly, has excused
me till to-morrow when I shall receive final instructions to
stay or go.

Let me say good night, sweet love, and I am certain I
will win you against the formidable opponent with which
[sic] I am faced.

God bless and guard you until we meet again. Sweetheart,
good night.

Yours ever,
Harry. xxx
xxxxx

1. Seán Ó Muirthuile, Gaelic League Organiser, secretary of the
Supreme Council of the IRB, and quartermaster general of the
National Army.

There is a playful element in the competition between
Collins and Boland for Kitty's affections, and Collins brings in
on his side an even closer friend, Gearóid O'Sullivan, the IRA's
adjutant-general, now also a member of the Dáil for Carlow-
Kilkenny. The friends Boland supped with at the Gresham

19

included two of Kitty's sisters, Maud or 'Mopsy' and Helen, E. J. Duggan, who was a senior member of Collins's intelligence organisation as well as the representative of Meath and Louth in the Dáil, and Seán Ó Muirthuile, the secretary of the Supreme Council of the IRB.

The exchange of letters with the British led ultimately to the appointment of five plenipotentiaries to a Conference in London whose purpose was 'to ascertain how the association of Ireland with the Commonwealth of Nations known as the British Empire could best be reconciled with Irish national aspirations'. Collins was one of the five. At that stage it was apparent that the best that could be done was to explore how close an approximation to a republic could be achieved. Lloyd George had earlier given de Valera a document outlining, with qualifications, the dominion status that existing members of the British Commonwealth enjoyed.

De Valera had decided not to lead the delegation, or to be one of its members, it being vital, he said, that his position as a symbol of the republic should be kept untouched. The plenipotentiaries were, therefore, to be led by Arthur Griffith. Their task, de Valera declared, might be beyond a mighty army and navy. Collins pressed de Valera to be part of the delegation; he did not want to go himself, he said, and would much prefer not to be chosen. De Valera replied that he would go were it not for his symbolic position; but it was absolutely essential that Collins should be a member of the delegation. From the personal touch and contact he had had with Collins's mind, he said, he felt and knew that his presence in the team was vital. He may also have thought that the British would not make their best offer in the absence of Collins. So Collins went to London without enthusiasm, and became more unhappy about his position as time went on. To the Supreme Council of the IRB, he said in November, 'I have been sent to London to do a thing which those who sent me know had to be done, but had not the courage to do themselves. We had not, when these terms were offered, an average of one round of ammunition for each weapon we had. The fighting area in Cork, which was the main area, was becoming daily more circumscribed, and they could not have carried on much longer.' (Ó Muirthuile memoir, P. 7/52). Preparations for the London conference added enormously to the burdens Collins was carrying. To get time for sleep was a problem.

Letter 12

Mícheál, Dublin, to Kitty, 29 September 1921.

My dear K,

I am scribbling you a hasty note just to say that I am alive. Are you? Do you know that to prove my scorn of a night without sleep I remained out of bed last night until 4 this morning. That's a bull. But it's useless, I'm getting too old! If you are still keeping up that hideous resolution of yours about *not* writing, I suppose I shall hear from you when I see you and not until then. Is it so, love?

Slán leat,
Mícheál.

This letter is a beauty, isn't it? Different *from everything.* Like to nothing. Am sending it to Maud, just so that she may know I am writing to you.

M.

'The Chief' (de Valera) had instructed Harry Boland to return to America, and the next two very sentimental letters reveal Boland's feelings as he resumes his journey.

Letter 13

Harry, Queen's Hotel, Cork to Kitty, 1 October 1921.

Pulse of my heart,

I'm here in Cork and feel just lonely and sad as the day itself, and God knows this is a real Cork day, raining soft and persistent!

I'm wondering if you are ever a wee bit lonely for me; and are you longing as I am for the day when we shall meet again? R.S.V.P.

How I can leave you even at the order of 'the Chief' I do not know, and I'm asking myself all the time if I have not made a great mistake in leaving you behind. Won't you send me a wireless to the *Celtic* and say you have made up your mind. If you have done so, cable *Yes*, and if you are still in doubt, then for God's sake try to make up your mind, and agree to come with me.

You will know by now that we have agreed to the Conference, but what may come of it I cannot say. We will know very soon if it is to be Peace or War. If Peace, I will be home in about six months. If war, I shall be in America until Dáil Éireann replaces me, and I would just love to have you come to America where we will spend our honeymoon in perfect bliss!

Mick and I spent the last night together. He saw me home at 2 a.m., and as I had to catch the 7.35 a.m. I bade him goodbye — only to find him at Kingsbridge as fresh as a daisy to see me off. I need not say to you how much I love him, and I know he has a warm spot in his heart for me, and I feel sure in no matter what manner our Triangle may work out, he and I shall be always friends.

I go to Cove in a few hours, and soon I shall feel the tang of the Western Ocean and open my lungs to its wonderful ozone. I am going back for the final phase of our work, and all the time I shall carry you with me in my heart, and now I want you to send me a little photo of yourself, one that I can carry in my match or cigarette case. Have a good long chat with Father Shanley, and do come back with him and marry me, after which we shall go to California for our honeymoon.

I have now to meet a gang of Corkonians who expect me to call on them ere I leave the Rebel City. So I bid you a fond farewell and, as I can not kiss you with my lips, I do so a million times with the lips of my heart.

May God bless and guard you,
Your devoted lover,
Harry.

Letter 14

Harry, Cove of Cork, to Kitty, 2 October 1921.

My dearest Kitty,

Here I am on the last leg of my journey. I arrived here last night from Cork city and soon I shall have 'the last glimpse of Erin'.

I want to say *Slán leat* to my own Kitty, and I wish you a very happy and pleasant time in Dublin next week. Write to me often and I shall be happy.

I must cut this short as I am in a hurry to catch the Mail. So farewell for a little time. May God guard you and direct you. Say a wee prayer now and then for your wandering Lover.

> Love without end,
> Harry.

He sent her a 'Goodbye, love' telegram as he sailed on 3 October, another as he passed Kerry, and from New York, on the 11th, he announced that he had 'arrived safe and well'. Harry's mother had somehow understood that his affair with Kitty was more advanced than it really was. She wrote a congratulatory letter.

Letter 15

K. Boland, 15 Marino Crescent, Clontarf to Kitty, 4 October 1921.

My dear Miss Kiernan,

Or shall I call you Kitty? As Harry tells me you are engaged to be married to him, allow me to congratulate you, and to wish every joy and blessing God can bestow on you both, for a better son never lived than Harry, also a loving brother, and I am confident he will be just as good a husband, for you know the old saying 'a good son makes a good husband'. Well, I feel sure he will be blest in his choice of a wife. Though I've not yet met you I have heard about you, and Kathleen[1] tells me she has met you and I don't wish to flatter you with all the nice things she said about you.

Well, dear, I hope to meet you next time you are in town, and sincerely trust you will come up to the Crescent so that we can know each other. Just let me know when you are coming to Dublin in case I might be out, which I would not wish for anything.

Harry's auntie and Kathleen join me in love and congratulations, and also hope to see you ere long in Dublin.

Very sincerely yours,
K. Boland, future mother-in-law.

1. Harry's sister.

———————————

But ten days later (14 October) Harry was writing to tell Kitty of not daring to tell his colleagues in America of his 'great hope', which was, of course, that Kitty, accepting his love for her, would come out to the States and marry him. Kitty would have had that letter about a week later. With Harry still hoping, Collins was displaying a markedly increased interest. On 5 October he told Kitty that he wanted her alone to come with him to the Prisoners' Fête (Letter 15A) and, on 14 October (Letter 23) he dealt with a doubt she had expressed that he might be more interested in somebody else by saying that 'You are the one — never fear'. Kitty then declares her love for him in the undated Letter 33. An 'arrangement' now exists which Collins speaks of making more binding later.

By that time one would expect that Kitty would have corrected the false impression Harry's mother had formed, and that she would have made it known to Harry that Collins, whom he had always recognised as a rival for her affections, was gaining on him. At any rate, one feels that she would have done something to avoid appearing to be encouraging the affections of both men simultaneously.

Letter 15A

Mícheál, Department of Finance, Dáil Éireann, to Kitty, 5 October 1921.

My dear Kitty,
   Would you come with me to the Shelbourne Park Fête (It's

the Prisoners' matter) tonight.[1] I want no one else but just yourself. If you can come I'll be at the Gresham at 8. If you can't come, I shall quite understand.

Yours,

M.

The children have not gone yet.

M.

1. One of many functions at that time to raise money for the prisoners and their dependents.

On the eve of his departure for the London Conference Collins scribbled a message to Kitty on a page from his loose-leaf note book.

Letter 16

Mícheál, Dublin or Greystones, to Kitty, 8 October 1921, at 11.50 p.m.

My very dear Kit,

Although circumstances forced me into the room before a late hour, I kept my promise and only opened your little note now. It was a delight.

May this cheer you up. Am working almost asleep. You'll forgive scribble therefore.

Can't write any more. Am thinking of you, and in a nice nice way.

God bless you. Hope you got home all right.

Eyes are closed, or almost.

Yours, I hope. Everything.

Mícheál.

Next day he wrote her a seven-page letter on Gresham Hotel notepaper, and scribbled a further note on a page of his note book. He has taught her how to spell Mícheál, the Irish form he obviously wishes her to use.

25

Letter 17

Mícheál, Gresham Hotel, Dublin, to Kitty, 9 October 1921.

My dear dear Kit,

This will be about the last act of mine before going away on the big venture. I am leaving in about half an hour's time and this must, therefore, be my farewell to you for a few days. Goodness knows I have a heavy heart this moment, but there is work to be done and I must not complain. The memory of the last few meetings — whatever comes — will be a pleasure and comfort to me. I had at last a good refreshing night's rest and I did more to-day in 2 or 3 hours than I have been able to do in *three times the time for many weeks.*

Twice during the night I woke — once I was positively talking aloud to you and I had some great thoughts about us which I'll tell you of some other time, and then the morning. One time of waking was 5 o'clock exactly.

You cannot know what a pleasure it was to me to feel you liked that little present. It will be a token of me to you, and if you think I forget, then listen to its little tick.

I feel today that arrangements of ours may be made more binding — do you think so?

If I write you to come to London you will, won't you? I won't do it unless I can see a fair time for you. One thing I would like to say finally is — that those few charming hours have placed on me while in London a restraint which I probably would not otherwise have felt. That is a good thing for me, and may be a good thing for our mission.

This page is the last. It is to say farewell. Even before you'd come to London, perhaps I could come home for a week-end and let you know myself.

With my fondest love and a sweet caress,
Mícheál.

He crossed to London on the night of Sunday, 9 October, arriving at Euston at 5.30 a.m. on Monday. That evening the newspapers had a story, allegedly from Collins himself, in which he boasted of having evaded discovery of his arrival.

He told Kitty: 'I never said any such thing. Newspapermen are inventions of the devil.' The Irish had taken two houses, 22 Hans Place, for most of the delegation and staff, and 15 Cadogan Gardens, Kensington where Collins intended to reside. He brought with him Emmet Dalton, Liam Tobin, Tom Cullen, Joe Guilfoyle, Joe Dolan, Ned Broy and Ned Barry. Miss O'Donoghue came over to be the house manageress, with 'Eddie', a waiter from the Gresham Hotel. Collins told Kitty that the presence of all these people made the place feel less strange.

The first meeting of the conference was to take place at 10 Downing Street on Tuesday, 11 October. That morning he scribbled a message to Kitty, 'Of all the times in God's world', he wrote, 'do you know when I'm writing this? Almost 4 o'clock in the morning.' And when no letter from Kitty came in the post, he sent her a telegram: 'Someone here very disappointed at not hearing. Fifteen Cadogan Gardens, Chelsea.'

As Mícheál and Kitty drew towards each other, poor Harry Boland, in the United States, awaited the reply to his appeal to Kitty to follow him out and marry him. He was still very hopeful that she would do so, as the next three communications show.

Letter 18

Harry, 411 5th Avenue, New York City, to Kitty, 11 October 1921.

A Chuisle mo Chroidhe,

This is my second day ashore. I'm writing to say that I missed yesterday's post. I was delighted to have your cable awaiting my return and I am eagerly looking forward to next Monday's mail to hear from you and praying that you will have written to say you are Coming!

All my old friends were at the Pier to meet me, and I met with a very hearty welcome. Saturday next I am being welcomed at a great mass meeting in Madison Square Gardens, and everything points towards a gathering of twenty thousand people being present. Frank P. Walsh and Senator La Folette[1] are to address the meeting with me. Mr O'Mara[2] and his wife are here in New York and are very happy. During my absence Mr O'Mara was in charge at Washington and did very well. Mrs O'Mara is a very lovely and charming girl and has made a great hit here. She has her sister with her for company and her name is Kitty! and like all Kittys she is lovely. We were out tonight sightseeing and I was thinking how nice 'twould be if you were here. Life would be so pleasant in this wonderful land. So come along at once like an angel and we will be for ever happy.

I wrote every day whilst at sea, and I'm wondering if you will read all the stuff I penned to you. I have many invitations to address meetings and I'm off to Washington on Monday next, after which I go to Chicago for Sunday 23 October. I will not go to California until you come, and as there is a pressing demand for me out there I put it up to you as a National Question to come at once. Seán Nunan[3] is in bed in the next room and desires remembrance to you. I bid you good night, sweetheart. May God bless and guard you is the prayer of

Your fond lover,
Harry.

1. Robert Marion La Folette (1855-1925), the distinguished Progressive Republican Senator from Wisconsin.
2. James O'Mara (1873-1948), a former Irish Party MP who embraced Sinn Féin in 1907. One of the trustees of the Dáil Éireann Loan. Went to the United States in 1920 to assist de Valera with the American end of the Loan operation. He brought with him his wife Agnes Cashel.
3. A 1916 man who was one of the clerks at the first public meeting of Dáil Éireann. Co-operated closely with de Valera in the United States. Was in later years the Irish Representative in Washington, and Secretary of the Department of Foreign Affairs.

Letter 19

Harry, 411 5th Avenue, New York City, to Kitty, 14 October 1921.

A Chuisle mo chroidhe,
    I'm writing to catch the mail to Europe to tell you that

I'm back on the job and in great shape. I have just written my speech for to-morrow's meeting of welcome so that you may read it, if you so desire. I am off to Washington on Sunday night where I shall remain until Saturday, 22 October, when I leave for Chicago to address a MacSwiney[1] memorial meeting on Sunday 23rd.

Mr and Mrs O'Mara have taken an apartment in Washington and I am to share it with them. This will suit me very well, and I will not be compelled to live in hotels. Of course I will be lonely until I know you are coming, and I will not give you an hour's rest until you have landed here.

The first week of the Conference in London has come and gone, and I am pleased to learn that all goes well so far. We shall soon know how the wind blows, whether the storms of war shall once again rage throughout our country or the gentle breezes of peace shall waft joy to our glorious land. I am going to write to Peggy's[2] mother to-night, altho' I may not be able to call on her until my return from Chicago. Seán Nunan and all the 'boys'[3] here are in great shape and are, of course, interested in you. I have not dared to tell them of my great hope, and I will spring your coming as a great surprise.

There's a heap of letters to sign right now ere we close down the mails and I close this hurried note with fond love to you, sweetheart.

Goodbye for a little while,

Your devoted lover,
Harry.

1. Terence MacSwiney.
2. Peggy Sheridan who married Larry Kiernan. She was an accomplished pianist and ofen played for Collins. *The Derry Air* was one of his favourite pieces.
3. 'The boys' in New York would have included Diarmuid Fawsitt and Gilbert Mac an Bháird.

Letter 20

Harry, Hotel Wolcott, 31st — 5th Avenue, New York City, to Kitty — a postcard, n.d.

My love,

A hurried note as I leave for Washington. Had a wonderful

welcome last night at Madison Square — was thinking of you all the time and wishing you were with me. Hurry along and enjoy the great Indian Summer in this wonderful land. I prayed on your beads at Mass this morning for you, and I know you said a wee prayer for me. Write to me often at 1045 or 411 — 5th.

> God Bless you.
> Your devoted lover,
> Harry.

Letters, which we have not got, came from Kitty and when Mícheál writes to her on 13 October, he refers to 'the arrangement' between them. Kitty raises the possibility that he may be interested in someone else. He disabuses her of the idea. He is confident that what they have planned will work out satisfactorily.

Her enquiring capricious mind is at work, and Mícheál takes her to task for the implications of one of her letters. Is she trying to get out of their commitment to each other? Later he apologises for being cross. 'It was a misunderstanding, the whole thing', she tells him, and she urges him to come to Granard and make it up. In a light-hearted note, of which we have a fragment, and which may fit in here, she presses for a week-end together. Mícheál by telegram suggests a meeting in the Gresham Hotel, Dublin for Saturday 22 October. Meanwhile, she goes to a dance and later gives Mícheál an account of it and of what she wore. It looks from the notes that follow that Collins, having made the hurried visit to Dublin, was seen off by her on the return journey. He writes to her from the mail boat, and again as soon as he reaches London.

Letter 21

Mícheal, London, to Kitty, 12 October 1921.

Kit dear,
   Have just returned from the Brompton Oratory. I was late for Mass a little, but the car hadn't come and I didn't know

30

the way very well. Lit a candle for you, a very big one. I
did the same yesterday morning.

After I had been to the Oratory yesterday I did a journey
of five miles to my sister's place for a letter from you — no
letter. Honestly, I felt it terribly, but I do not believe that
you have failed to write, and won't believe it until I know.

Saw Helen[1] and Paul[2] last night. We had quite a little
party. These two, Seán Ó Muirthuile, Mr & Mrs Duggan, self
and my sister. Had dinner with Helen and Paul and went to a
show afterwards. I'd have given anything to have had you
there. Alas!

I kind of told Helen. I fancy they'd all be very pleased —
What do you think?

Good-bye for the day. Tough work before me. Every good
wish and thought.

Mícheál.

And also sent a telegram.

1. Helen Kiernan, and 2. Paul McGovern were on their honeymoon.

Letter 22

Mícheál, London, to Kitty, 13 October 1921.

Kit dearest,

You will know from my wire yesterday that I had got into
a state of great concern about not hearing from you. Now
I'm all right as I have got your letters. They arrived late last
night and I picked them up after Mass this morning. Even if
yours had not come I'd write you this morning. This must be
short, although there are many things I'd like to say. However, you know what I have on hand just now, and I want
you to know that you are in my mind, and I think of you
every moment I am free.

I was in a queer mood on Tuesday (probably a bit
unstrung) when I wrote that — what must appear to you to
be a hectoring letter. Yet I'll say nothing more of it. You will
often be called on to stand a lot from me also. But then
straightforwardness and understanding.

No, don't think I resent your sermon. It's a queer thing but I feel very like that, and I have often felt that it required some one like you to make me appreciate the thing properly. I must say that I feel appreciation coming.

You'll be glad to know that I'm sleeping and keep in very good form. This is really true, and I tell you so that you won't be worrying. Now another thing — what I meant by restraint was less excitement, earlier hours, not just your meaning. It has worked out, and *you've done it*. I really liked your letters. Always write as you feel, to me at any rate. I'll do the same to you.

I have lighted a candle for you at the Brompton Oratory each morning.

Of course I paid that 3d.

Why did you send me back the £1.

> With all my love,
> Mícheál.

I was so glad you liked that note written in the Gresham [on 9 October]. That was most spontaneous on my part and came from a very great longing. We *must*, I think, make that arrangement more binding, but just as you desire. I feel somehow that it will work out and work out well.

> Slán leat,[1]
> M.

1. Good-bye.

Letter 23

Mícheál, London, to Kitty, 14 October 1921.

My dear dear Kit,

This note is certainly going to be short. Several people waiting for me and a conference at 11. Have just come back from Mass. Lit a candle for you as I do each morning.

I don't know how many times I have read your letter. It's awfully good, and I do really love it. Your *rebuke* — for it is just ever so little a rebuke — about someone else who would really be the one is a little upsetting. You don't mean it like that tho', I'm sure. You are the one — never fear. How

I wish I could see you now and have one of those lovely serious talks with you. They are the best ones, aren't they? Parts of your letter were somewhat like them.

You'll never know what good that letter did me yesterday — it helped me all through the day, and it was one of the hardest days we have yet had. At it from early morning until 8 almost and you don't know what an ordeal that is.

Slán leat for the day. Am looking forward to a letter in half an hour. God be with you.

Fondest love,
M.

Do you like my letters or only some of them?

Letter 24

Mícheál, London, to Kitty, fragment of letter, Friday night, very late, and Saturday afternoon, 14 and 15 October 1921.

Kitty my dear,

I got your letters to-day at the lunch adjournment from the Conference. They were very lovable, and I've read them many times since. All the evening I've been in working — just went out for a short walk at 10.45 and back now 11.15. Interesting news, isn't it? But I want to tell you. No one else in the house or in the other house,[1] I envy them — they can go away, but I must stay. My own fault I suppose.

Well, my dear dear Kit, I do think I am quite certain of the relationship and I just loved the way you stated the case. So like you — I'm always thinking now that we shall get on better and better — what do you think?

You asked me if I really wore the tie? Look at the photograph and the distinctive stripe. Could anything be plainer?

Got to this point last night before going to bed and now I'm resuming at 4.15 in the afternoon after a fearful hard slogging day. Started at the usual time — Mass at 8, but, although I'm beginning to feel tired now, I'm feeling happy also for all my arrears of work have disappeared and I'm in pretty clear water again.

Well, I must deal with your letters as best I can.

With regards to coming to London, if H and P[2] are here
for a few days, why couldn't you do it? You wouldn't
get very much attention, I'm afraid, but you'd be here and
that would be the great thing. Please yourself however. I'd
just love to have you here even if only for a few days. But
above all don't stand out against a natural inclination —
sure you won't?

Then the next point — it won't change now, I'm sure. We
must have a talk about it as soon as we meet. I believe it will
be splendid. As long as I know you want to be. . . .

[Note across top of letter: 'Crowne's[3] letter returned. God
help him. He'd be foolish to look me up, however. M.']

1. 22 Hans Place.
2. Helen and Paul.
3. It has not been possible to establish who this was. Could it have been
someone named Browne?

Letter 25

*Mícheál, 15 Cadogan Gardens, Chelsea, London S.W., to
Kitty, n.d.*
[In a note at the head of the paper he announces, 'Today
is my birthday. Only one who remembered it was my sister,
the nun.[1] She sent me the enclosed and I send it to you with
every wish she has for me. M.' This fixes the date of the letter
as 16 October 1921. It is a Sunday.]

Kit dear,
Following on last night's note I am now acknowledging
your letter written on Thursday at 1.30. It is afternoon —
a lovely day — bells ringing for Church and Chapel — sunshine
on my left, typewriters clacking on my right. I have kept the
lovely secretaries in working, and it's a shame for me, but alas
I have to do it.

Curious thing I have just come in from meeting a man
named Collins. He says his father came from Granard. I knew
some Collins's must have been there before, and how I wish
I were there now — on the Moat.[2] Last time I was on the
Moat, early morning. Do you remember? I looked across the
Inny to Derryvaragh over Kinali and Sheelin (and thought of

Fergus O'Farrell[3]) to Mount Nugent and turning westward
saw Cairnhill where the beacons were lighted to announce to
the men of Longford that the French had landed at Killala.[4]
Queer how I run off like this, especially when you are not
interested in these things.

Was at two Masses today! One my usual at the Oratory
8 o'c. The other an official one at Maiden Lane. Even at
the official one I managed to come back and light a candle
for *you*. Second one *therefore*, today. Dr MacRory[5]
celebrated the Mass and we paid our respects to him afterwards. We were photographed and, if you ever see the
photograph, you'll see your *second* tie.

Now as to your own letter — one thing I was glad to hear
and that was the light comfort you got through my not
believing you hadn't written. Well, wasn't I right? I had
even thought of the tired Sunday and the worked Monday,
so even through my disappointment I had my explanation.

H and P looked fine. There is no mistake there, I'm happy
to say. Isn't that good? I feel exactly like you about it — the
aftermath. That's the first test. Every test passed is another
milestone on the way to life-long happiness. My sister[6]
liked them both very much indeed. She didn't know that
Helen was the girl I mentioned to her once, and she didn't
know that you were her sister. She'll like you — don't worry
about that. Yes, it was a lovely party, but I was unpleasant,
as I have really too many things to carry out at the present
moment. It is not right for me to inflict myself on people.

Please always say to me what you think, not what I'd
like you to think. That's the only way to get at a proper
understanding, and if I don't like what you say, then it's
my look out. You realise what I mean — don't you, Kit?
And I hope you'll see a close link when you look at the real
photograph and see the more vivid stripes.

It must have been nice for you to see the children doing
yourself. Tell me more about it. Were they doing you in love
or in _ _ _ but no, they could only love you. I hope some
one of them thought of me.

You'll have seen all the praise and flattery that has been
showered on me since I came here and have been publicly
known. You will know I hope that they leave me untouched

35

just as their dispraise and their blame did. All the same to me. That upper lip of mine has been called on to do much scornful upturning since I've seen you.

> God bless and protect you
> Dear dear Kit
> M.

Please excuse the frightful length of these things,

> M.

1. Helen Collins, Sister M. Celestine.
2. The Moat. At one end of Granard, where the town's churches are situated, there is an elevated land mass, known to antiquarians as a motte-and-bailey, that dates back to the twelfth century.
3. O'Farrell, the leader of the Irish insurgents in the Granard area.
4. The French under Humbert landed at Killala on 22 August 1798, and with Irish recruits had a considerable initial success at Castlebar. Hope of a general rising was vain, however, and, to avoid a too early conflict with Cornwallis's and Lake's overwhelming forces, Humbert turned across country towards Granard where he was led to believe an insurrection had broken out. The campaign ended in disaster for the invaders at Ballinamuck. The surrender of the French was accepted, but the unfortunate Irish were excluded from quarter, and cut down without mercy.
5. Joseph MacRory, D.D., Bishop of Down and Connor.
6. Hannie.

Letter 26

Mícheál, London, to Kitty, 17 October 1921.

Kitty dear,

Just a line — only a line to wish you well and to let you know I am thinking of you.

Yesterday's photograph has been published, I am told — *Nervous Michael Collins*. However, I have received no cuttings yet. Too early, but I fear there will be no chance of writing later in the day.

> With my fond fond love,
> Mícheál.

Letter 27

Kitty, to Mícheál, Monday morning, n.d.

My very dear Mícheál,

There was no post going out here yesterday, so I hope you won't be disappointed at not getting a letter today. It seems ages since I heard from you, and needn't say I'm looking forward to the post to-day. It also seems a long time now since I was speaking to you.

I wonder how you are doing in London? Meet any nice girls that you liked? Did you kiss anybody since? I didn't — didn't get the chance (You know I'm only joking!). I too wish that I could see you, to have one of those great little chats. They certainly are great. Wonder how I'd be if I could just meet you now. Perhaps I'd be quite disappointing, but you'd understand and wouldn't mind. You know I'm a moody creature sometimes, but I don't think you are. I always find you the same as far as I'm concerned, and I'm glad, as I'd probably misunderstand you otherwise. Another thing: you are just yourself when with me. I wonder if I'm always myself with you. Of course I do want to be.

Maud, Doc and myself were away for a long drive yesterday and, of course, I was thinking of you most of the time and wondering what you would be doing on a Sunday.

I prayed for you at Mass. I love you to light a candle for me, too, but I started it! Would you ever have thought of it?

The Dr has just come in, and came straight over to try and kiss me 'good morning'. I had to laugh and said 'No', for, as I've just said, I kiss no one! He took it well and went away. Funny, wasn't it, in the middle of my letter?

I'll write you a long letter tonight, if I don't feel too tired after the market . . . . Will keep all news until then. I'm rushing now. Have to go down to the shop.

My love to you,

Kit.

Letter 28

Mícheál, 15 Cadogan Gardens, Chelsea, London S.W. to Kitty, 19 October 1921.

My dear Kitty,

I was cross — very cross — when I wrote yesterday. I tried hard all day to forget you, but it wouldn't work out. I gave up the attempt and I punished myself for not being nice to you — and there you are. *You* have it all now. That being so, I hope you won't feel it necessary to write any more severe letters.

Got your Monday [morning] letter last night when I called to my sister's place. Didn't get on too well with her either. Trouble everywhere. My own fault. One thing in your letter is truly fine. It does seem ages since I saw you! And it does seem a long way — to our next conversation I mean. These conversations are fine, and they are straight, *and that's that.*

Hope you enjoyed that drive. Last night I escaped from all my people and went for a drive alone. Rather funny — the great M.C. in lonely splendour. I am lonely actually and I suppose you won't believe that, and *that's that.*

Sorry that some of my letters should fall short. Read those ones again. They are not meant to fall really short. But life has to take in the serious things as well as the light things, and even though we may like sunshine always, it is not practical nor indeed — and remember this — is it desirable. And that's that.

And I am very cross with myself this morning, and I am very apologetic to you and I ought to be, and not for yesterday's letter merely but a lot more, and without you I would never have thought of the candles and I know I owe you any amount, and I know that you have been of immense help to me and I was overjoyed last night when my sister asked when were P and H returning from Paris, and couldn't we have dinner with them and perhaps K. could be there also. I wonder if K.[1] would, and I wonder what my K. thinks of this letter. It's very unlike me, isn't it? And I won't change it, and slán leat and everything.

And this is finished,
And love & blessings,
Mícheál.

And I have never asked for M[2] and Vi[3] and I do think of them. So tell them. And Mrs Duggan asks for you and everything. M.

1. Kitty, of course.
2. Her sister Maud.
3. Violet Davis, a daughter of the manager of the Ulster Bank in Granard. She married the Paul Cusack who designed clothes for the Kiernan girls.

Letter 29

Mícheál, London, to Kitty, 20 October 1921.

Kitty dear,

This is to answer yours of Monday evening. I have a kind of idea that I ought really return that letter and let you look at it, and compare it with this reply, for I'll try this time to reply solidly to all your points. But, first of all, don't be putting up too severe tests. Don't attempt to walk before we have learned to crawl. That is a fatal mistake. It is something that can't be done.

By the bye, first of all — do you know how your letter strikes me, I mean in net substance? It is this, that *you* are trying to get out of it. Is this really so? I don't want to get out of it. I want it to work out and I promise to do my part of it. If it's not possible, then God help us, but let us have a fair chance. Isn't that right? Last night H[1] asked me if she could do anything for us. I said no — we have to get this thing settled ourselves. Isn't that right also?

You were not forgotten, and if my letter had not reached you at all, you should know that you were not forgotten, and, if I were in jail and couldn't write to you at all, you should also know that you were not forgotten. I knew I wasn't and that in spite of your not writing — actually not writing — for two days; and, if you only knew the difficulty I have in finding time, you'd know how unfair you were to talk of long letters. (Since I commenced this, I have had to deal with several business letters, a few callers and a few phone calls.) I don't find it difficult to write you a long letter — I want to write to you all day really — but I have many obligations, and don't forget that, even in the midst of them, I didn't let two days pass without writing. But I mustn't mind, must I? However, *perhaps* I do mind. And I'm not going to be cross any more, and that's that, and I'm not in good form any longer, and I wasn't able to get to bed until 3 o'c this morning, and I was up at 7.15 to go to the Oratory, and that's that, and I'm sorry if I may be appearing to be unpleasant to you. And it's my real friends that have to suffer these things, and please don't *you* blame me.

Don't be disappointed about the other thing. I don't want to be a hypocrite about it or anything else. I'm getting into that direction. Will you leave it at that for the moment?

All the company are well. I think they liked your enquiry. Poor Sheila[2] was enchanted. Everybody likes you. That's not good luck for me, also. I hope you have written to Mrs D.[3] I'm making her life a misery at the present time, but again it's a case of my real friends.

Will you really come here? Very likely you would not see too much of me. Don't you think that the seeing part of it has gone a good deal deeper now? I regard your attitude as being correct. If the contract be entered into, it is only just that the terms shall be kept. Isn't that right? I do understand you — whatever else you make a mistake about, don't make any mistake about that. And perhaps it is you who would feel different next year, and haven't we to chance that too? And if you *really* think I don't consider these things, and if you *really* do trust such a thing lightly, then you know nothing about me. And in spite of it, I would not change a word in your letter for I don't like gramaphone effects. I like people to say what they themselves think and mean.

Were we really criticised? And by whom? So much the worse for the critics! Don't mind them. That was the thing — we ought to have been away from everybody. When we were, there was no necessity for criticism. Isn't that right also? By the bye, do you really think I'd laugh over it now? Were my explanations so utterly bad? You need not dread our next meeting. I look forward to it more eagerly than ever before. And, finally, you are right — If it can't last through misfortune and trouble and difficulty and unpleasantness and age then it's no use. In riches and beauty and pleasure it is so easy to be quite all right. That is no test though.

> Goodbye Kit and every good wish for the day,
> M.

Look at the enclosed. Please destroy it as it may be regarded
as a breach of confidence. It is not though, really.

> Yours,
> M.

1. Helen.
2. Sheila's identity has not been established.
3. Mrs Duggan.

Letter 30

Mícheál, London, to Kitty, 21 October 1921.

Kit,

Good morning — have you used Pears Soap?[1]

Have been working all the morning and now I'm rushing
for the Conference. Am keeping them late *as usual*, they say,
and you say I'm neglectful and forgetful if I don't write long
letters and so I'm getting into trouble everywhere and that's
always my fate. Your pencilled note was very hard to read
but I liked it very much.

And there you are and good bye and fond love and
everything.

> Mícheál.

1. A catch phrase of the period.

Letter 31

Kitty, to Mícheál, Wednesday, n.d.

[In pencil, 'Written on my knee in shop, so excuse'.]

My very dear Mícheál,

I am surprised at your note just received. I never meant
you to read my letter the way you did. Never suggested that
you were not straight in any one of the things you suggested.
I'm afraid you took the letter all wrong.

I am very sorry if I have offended you, or made you unhappy by that letter — and really you probably won't believe me, but it was never intended as such. I can't remember the letter exactly now, but am quite sure that, when writing it, I didn't feel those things. As I do now, always did, you are everything to me, and surely you know it. Then why should I want to hurt you? No, you misjudge me. It was a misunderstanding, the whole thing, and I am sorry. Please forget it and remember that I am always thinking of you. You are never out of my heart. I feel very sad and unhappy today since I got your note. Do hope that my next one will cheer you, and have a different effect. Will be more careful next time what I write! My letters are slow going. Wrote on Monday, you should have it Tuesday night.

It worries me and it is always worrying that you have so much to do. Is there no remedy? I wish I was near you now. Come for the week-end. Ah, do. *This* week-end. Couldn't be done? How I'd love it. Ah, yes try, try. You will come. Just send a note Friday that you are coming Saturday.

I wrote you, or tried to write you a nice letter yesterday. Hope it will please you and help to lighten the heavy load.

This is my morning in shop. Then I go over in the evening[1] in such bad bad humour, to try to wash my hair for the night, sew my long frock etc. Your note has upset it all. But I'll go to the dance. That's what you would like me to do, isn't it? But this doesn't say I'll enjoy it. You, of course, will be near all the time. I'll feel that I'll want to talk of you always, but it might bore other men! That isn't the way to get partners at a Ball! So I'll just have to put my best foot forward if I want to dance. Had a nice little note come from you, I'd be in great form going. Larry is motoring me.

I wish that you were here, and please make it up with me and don't be vexed. Send me a wire if you have time. I'll know by it that all is well.

Can't you be more kind to yourself as regards work, and have more sleep and air. You never hint how things are going over there, but suppose it's hard to tell.

Went to bed real early last night and prayed for you.

Was the letter awful that you destroyed? Did you say

42

good-bye to me for good. I'd forgive you if you did it just in a fit. Write and say we are as great as ever. Your letter today was not like you, nor like the lovely ones that I got before.

If my letter written on Monday night displeases you, it was partly Dr MacM's fault. He tried to tease me all the time, firing things at me while I was writing it. I got into a temper.

Good-bye with my love and a big kiss (if you'll have it).

Yours ever,
Kit.

[Later, written in flat]

Please excuse bad writing and pencil, and please write and say if you are still cross with me. You knew well that that letter of yours would make me very unhappy and mine has made you unhappy. If I had thought you were tired and worn out I would probably have been more careful. Dear dear sweetheart, you know that I want to be a little help to you especially under those conditions. I am more than sorry that I was just the opposite. Please give me the chance of making it up to you.

I send you a big hug as well as a kiss with my love.

Your own little pet,

1. To the hotel.

Letter 32

Kitty to Mícheál, a fragment, n.d.

. . . I love to have you here, but we must be really good, no bedroom scene etc. etc. etc. Tuigeann tú?[1] You'll come to me before I go to London perhaps? Unfortunately I'm rushing this for post. Feel in great form for writing, but you won't get it tomorrow, if I wait. You know country posts.

I'm off to a dance in Cavan tomorrow D.V. My first for ages. A boy (aged 17) called yesterday here to know if he could take me to it. He is from there, and, says he, 'I've

missed you from all the dances this long time, and now you'll
have to come'. He's only a kid, dances well and has a great
grádh[2] for me. I'll tell you about the dance after it. Larry
etc. may go too. I'm wearing my old long frock, black and
very low! Of course *you* would be shocked!

Thanks for the Little Flower.[3] I'll pray to her. Saw Mass
pictures in *Sketch*. You have still the Charlie Chaplin
moustache![4] Have heaps to say to you when we do meet
soon.

1. Do you understand?
2. affection.
3. The Carmelite nun Thérèse Martin of Lisieux, whose canonis-
   ation was being widely advocated.
4. For a short time Mícheál had a moustache, but not of the Charlie
   Chaplin kind, and a number of photographs have survived showing
   him with one.

Letter 33

Kitty to Mícheál, Thursday, n.d.

My dear M,
   This won't be a letter anyway as I'm half dead after the
dance, but just to show you that I didn't forget. No letter
from you today. It's the first time I've got this to say, and
to let you see I'm not vexed, exactly.

   Went to bed for 2 hours this morning. Couldn't sleep.
So I'm in the shop now.

   The dance was stunning. I had a great time. Wore my old
black evening dress, held up on shoulders by two little black
straps and will power, no sleeves, long draped skirt with a
small slit in front. I felt I never looked so well and was
wishing that you were here to tell me if you liked me. Oh I
forgot, a large red flower on dress, a string of red beads and
a red hankie. With my watch I looked *it*. Sorry for such a
bad description of myself, but am very sleepy and tired.
You like black in evening dresses. It suits me, I think.

   Are you still vexed with me? I suppose, when you get one
or two letters, written at the end of the week, about your
photo, you'll be mad. But half the time I'm only joking
about your cruel face which I heard somebody else say.

44

Don't always think that I mean just everything. It's my rotten mean way of trying to get you to say you won't be cross, and that I'm your little pet.

Last night I was yours absolutely, that is if *you* were perfectly satisfied. All night I danced, danced, never sat out for a second, never felt inclined; and, with so much dancing, I do feel more tired. About 50 times I danced, with encores of course. My second dance was with a Co. Inspector R.I.C., a grey-haired man who was in love with my mother. Started telling me I was like her and so on. Funny isn't it?

Well, how are you? I wish that I had never worried you, because it probably had a bad effect on you, made you think unkind things of me. And I suppose you had to get some ladies over there, secretaries for instance, to amuse you, to provide a little diversion from all the work. That's why I am not sorry that I gave you the opportunity by my behaviour. I only say 'I suppose'; forgive my supposing. Perhaps you don't bother. I hope not.

My hand is getting cold. I can't write, but I want you to know that I love you. I love you oh so much. When can we meet? Pity our first hour was so serious. I'll not fall out with you again, even if *you* want to. Until we meet at least once again,

K.

Letter 34

Mícheál, on way to London, to Kitty, Sunday 23 October 1921.

Kit,

At the time I'm writing this you are just about back to the Gresham, that is if Pat Mc[1] hasn't killed you all. Would you believe that I'm awfully cross with myself just now, thinking how much nicer I ought to have been to you. I hope all my lads did see you home safely.

Boat rocking badly. God bless my Kit and keep her safe.

Love,
M.

To my own little *pet*. Enclosure for Dr Farnan.[2] Would you mind explaining to him that I'm writing on a rocky boat? I'm hard set to keep sitting up.

Enclosure

To Dr R. Farnan,
5 Merrion Sq
23 October 1921

My dear Dr Farnan,
The bearer of this note is Miss K. Kiernan — a friend of mine. She says probably unjustly that there is something wrong with her. I wonder if you'd mind seeing her and advising. Someone mentioned your name to her and she happened to mention the matter to me so I said I'd write you a note. This is written on a very rolling boat, and you'll know [*sic*]. My love to Mrs F.

Best wishes,
M. Ó Coileáin.

1. Pat McCrea who drove for Collins sometimes.
2. Dr Robert Farnan, a friend of the movement and particularly of de Valera, who resided at 5 Merrion Square. Member of Seanad Éireann later.

Letter 35

Mícheál, London, to Kitty, 23 October 1921.

Kit, Kit,
I wish you were with me now. It's so lonely, and it's so sad being far away. But then you *are* with me, aren't you? Why wasn't I so much nicer to you. Good bye Kit, my Kit.

M.

Boat heaving like anything. Difficult to write.

Letter 36

Mícheál, London, to Kitty, 24 October 1921.

Kit, my dear Kit,
Am hastily scribbling a note before going out to Mass. I

know there will be no chance afterwards, for I already see ominous signs of work here. I wonder if you're sleeping soundly at this moment, or are just awake and thinking of me. It's 7.50.

We had a good journey and slept on in the train until just now.[1] Home to shave and now I'm off out.

How do you feel about it all this morning? Did you really enjoy yesterday? I do wish I had been nicer to you, but perhaps I wasn't too bad altogether.

Slán leat for the day,
With my fondest love,
Mícheál.

1. The morning mail reached Euston at about 5.30 but passengers, exceptionally, could stay on for a couple of hours.

Mícheál, in London, reads Kitty's letter about the dance and her outfit. He has begun to worry about the state of her health, which he had discussed with her in Dublin. 'I am thinking of those grey hairs'.

Letter 37

Mícheál, London, to Kitty again, 24 October 1921.

Kit dearest,

I'm absolutely crazy, you'll say, to sit down to write you twice in one day. Perhaps I am. There is a reason though. I have received your letter written on Thursday. You must have been 'stunning' looking in that outfit right enough. Sounded somewhat on the naked side in reality, but I can scarcely think it was so. It wasn't a letter anyway as you very properly say. Did you explain that you got that letter of mine? Have you been too busy today to write one? Did you go home by the early morning train? Or did you go home at all?

I hope you'll go to Dr F, or if you don't like going to him, what about Dr Hayden, Dr O'Brien or Dr John Ryan? Also about your sight — would it not be well to go to Dr Cummins?[1]

You see I have begun taking real care of you, and you must take real care of your self. I am thinking of those grey hairs today. Glad there is something I can reproach you about. I'm greatly afraid though you have me completely in this way.

Would you look at the enclosed. It needs no restraint on my part whoever she is. Lit a candle for you. Slán leat.

I'll write — or wire tomorrow about coming over.

M.

[He, or Mrs E. J. Duggan for him, sent her a telegram later that day.]

1. These were all well-known Dublin doctors at that time.

Arrangements are made for her visit to London. Mrs E. J. Duggan who, with Mrs Fionan Lynch, was looking after the girls on the delegation, wired her on 24 October: 'I wonder if you could come over to-morrow crossing at night. You could arrive Euston 5.31 morning, leaving Westland Row 7.10. Would meet you Euston with car if travelling. Report and wire Gearóid [O'Sullivan] and get a sleeper. Wire me to-morrow early. Urgent.' On the following day Mary Duggan wired again, twice:

(1) If you can, come tomorrow Wednesday. There is not the slightest use after that. Cross Wednesday night or not at all, and wire early to-morrow morning. Please do come.

(2) Further to other wire. Perhaps you could travel day-time tomorrow, if you come to Dublin this evening.

Kitty went over, probably on 26 October, but we know little more than that. However, Kathleen McKenna, who was one of the four secretary-typists to the delegation, noted that the two Kiernans who came to see Mícheál in London — Kitty, and Helen on her honeymoon — were very attractive girls and that Mícheál very proudly walked out of Cadogan Gardens one day with one of them on each arm. He was 'very much in love with Kitty'. That is evident from the care Mícheál took of the arrangements for the return journey.

By the end of October the major issues on which it was likely agreement would be difficult had been raised at the

48

Conference. These were the unity of Ireland, allegiance to the Crown, common citizenship, naval defence, the national debt, war pensions, compensation, and tariffs. None of these matters were mentioned by Collins in his letters to Kitty. He was unable to do so, even if he thought she would be interested, for, like all the participants in the Conference, he was under an obligation to maintain secrecy. To those who were involved, however, it was evident that the Irish were prepared to accept a free partnership with the other states of the British Commonwealth and to recognise the Crown as head of the association, but leaving open for further discussion the form in which this was to be done. The Irish insisted on the essential unity of Ireland, and it was here the crunch came. Craig, now the Prime Minister of a Northern Ireland government, refused to budge an inch on this question and as the British were unable or unwilling to force him, a break in the negotiations threatened by 8 November. Mícheál 'was obviously very upset' (Jones, 155/6); but when he tells Kitty that he is 'very, very discontented', he may be referring to his unhappy relations with Dublin.

During November 1921 Kitty wrote as usual but none of her letters for that month are in the collection. We are dependent, therefore, for November on the following unbroken sequence from Mícheál who spent most of that month in London. He manages a week-end visit to Granard, sends her a wire from Dublin on the way back, and writes a long letter when he gets to London. But, though he has to return for other meetings in Dublin, that's the only time they see each other during the month. Mícheál complains of the reproachful tone of Kitty's letters; and describes Harry Boland's 'storming' of Kitty as 'unfair'.

The 'storming' suggests that in a competition for Kitty's affections Harry was not prepared to concede victory to Collins without a struggle. What form that took we don't know, nor do we know why Collins should have considered that in this regard Harry was acting unfairly. That the 'storming' was done essentially by Boland himself, who was in America all this time, must be assumed, but unfortunately there are none of his letters and telegrams among the correspondence. Other people may have intervened on Harry's behalf at his prompting, but that is unlikely; and we have been unable to verify an equally unlikely story that de Valera tried to influence Kitty's decision as between her two suitors.

Collins agreed to have his portrait painted by Sir John Lavery and found the experience of sitting still 'absolute torture'. Lavery (pp. 214-15) thought he was 'a patient sitter', however, but noticed that Collins, always on the alert, liked to sit facing the door.

At the Conference things were 'hotting up'. 'We're getting into the heart of things now', he told Kitty on 16 November. The area of disagreement became wider on 22 November when the Irish handed in their comments on the first draft of a Treaty the British had prepared, prefacing them with a note emphasising that the essential unity of Ireland must be maintained. Their position on the source of legislative and executive authority, their desire to confine association with the Commonwealth to purposes of common concern, to limit the recognition of the Crown to being the symbol and accepted head of the association, and their views on naval defence left Lloyd George with the general impression that the Irish delegates had returned to their original notion of a totally independent state. He was filled with despair, he said. Were the Irish to be in the Commonwealth or not? De Valera's idea of external association which had been introduced into the discussion, first by Collins, was unacceptable. It seemed so evident that a break was in sight that the departments of the Dáil were advised to be ready for a resumption of the war. At this critical point Mícheál wrote Kitty a letter of which a disjointed page and the last few lines have survived.

Through the good offices of two British civil servants, Tom Jones of the cabinet secretariat and Alfred Cope of the Chief Secretary's Office, Dublin, contact was renewed between the delegations. Collins crossed to Ireland on the night of Thursday 24 November with Griffith and talked things over in the Dáil cabinet on the 25th, without being 'much richer in expedients' (Pakenham, 199). He then went down to Granard, but was back in Dublin on the morning of Monday the 28th and in London on the 30th. Between

then and the evening of Friday 2 December, the situation
was clarified and improved for the Irish on a number of
points, and a second draft of the Treaty was prepared. This
was taken by the Irish delegation to Dublin for 'a confused
and inconclusive discussion' (Jones, 179) on Saturday,
3 December. Collins had told a friend in London a little
earlier that he did not know whether the delegation was
'being instructed or confused' from Dublin, and he added
'the latter I would say' (Taylor, 132).

Letter 38

Mícheál, London, to Kitty, 25 October 1921.

Kitty dear,
    I wired you last night asking if you'd come over. Am
looking forward to getting a reply anytime now. I hope
so much that you really will come.
    Today I saw by a note from Gearóid[1] that you received
a cut on Sunday evening. You never told me and you never
pretended. Hope Tom[2] saw you back all right, but I'm sure
he did.
    Am not writing this as a letter and not intending that it
should be a letter. It is written in case you could not come,
and to show you that I'm thinking of you. Goodness knows I
am.

Beannacht Dé leat,[3]
Mícheál.

1. Gearóid O'Sullivan.
2. Tom Cullen.
3. God be with you.

Letter 39

*Mícheál, 15 Cadogan Gardens, London, to Kitty, n.d., at
12.30 a.m.*

My dear dear Kit,
    I have just said that rosary for you and I must write this
note just to let you [know] that I am wondering how you

are, and where you are on the journey? Somewhere near
Crewe? Have you written anything sooner than this and,
if you have, you're a marvel. I do hope you are having a nice
journey, and that they'll attend to you well at Holyhead. Do
you remember our words about my being sorry that I hadn't
been nice to you? Well I must say it again, for it is only now
I realise how unpleasant it was and I pray you not to be too
hard on me for you know how difficult my task is and, as I
said before, I visit my nastiness on my best friends.

@ 9 a.m.

About this time I hope Gearóid will be taking you away from
Dunleary and I am so anxious to know if you had a nice
journey and if you were attended to properly. Had you any
trouble at Holyhead and what kind was the sea crossing? I am
also wondering to know if Gearóid has really and truly met
you, but somehow I feel it will be all right. Whatever I did to
you or forgot to do I tried to make up for it by being nice at
the end, but I'm afraid that was too late to really make up —
was it?

Hope you'll get all your business done satisfactorily in
Dublin today. As I write this there is a possibility that I may
cross tonight but even so it will only be a crowded week-end.
I'll know only at about 5 this evening.

Am writing this under difficulty before breakfast having
just come in from St Mary's.[1] Said a "word" for you, and lit
a candle. Goodbye my dear Kit with

Fondest love from,
Mícheál.

1. A church on Hammersmith Road.

Letter 40

Mícheál, London, to Kitty, 8 November 1921.

Dearest Kit,

Have got here safely — arrived No. 15 a few minutes after
5.30. Crossing extremely rough but we did not feel it —
actually I had a large dinner on the boat. Slept practically

the whole way on the train, turned in for about 2 hours here, up at 7.30, Mass at 8 and now I'm writing this before breakfast. You'll be glad to know that I'm feeling tip top but I am lonely, and very very discontented. You needn't ask if I thought of you at Mass and a candle — yes indeed and I'm thinking so very much of you now.

The week-end (notwithstanding my own unpleasantness) did me a great deal of good. The constant and changing fresh air was a great tonic. Yesterday morning's journey back was lovely. Very cold, but I didn't really feel that. Practically the whole way I was lost in admiration of the view. The various colourings of the leaves were beautiful in the extreme and as we came in view of Lough Owel the sun — which seemed to have caught all the waters as if in a saucer — shone brilliantly on the lake and transformed it into a glimmering silver. Really I never thought things looked so lovely. I wonder why? Perhaps it was that I was happy and yet I kept thinking of that parting message of yours about the pity — you do misjudge me there. I could not have expressed myself properly I'm afraid. It is only that I do understand some of those inevitable things and I do hope I didn't seem unkind.

How did you get on yesterday? Granard market is held on an ill-chosen date. Monday — how could anyone be in proper mood or manner for buying and selling on a Monday morning? Of course this is the real explanation of the late hour of starting — isn't it? Anyway I hope the day was not very strenuous for you and that you got through all right. Let me know please.

As usual when I got back to town there were several people looking for me and a meeting. Then of course I became remorseful and blamed myself for not having started in proper time, but that had to be got over also.

Are you thinking of me now? And how are you feeling about it all? When do you come to town again? That's important! Do you understand?

Must go to breakfast. Good-bye for today with all my love and every blessing to my Kit.

Mícheál.

Letter 41

Mícheál, 15 Cadogan Gardens, London, to Kitty, 9 November 1921.

Kitty dearest,

This will be a very very short note I fear as there is already a clamour for me to attend to certain things but I can afford to let them wait for a while as I'm well up with things again. I let everybody go off last night and stayed alone in the house. Worked steadily for three or four hours — was not disturbed until about 10.30 and at that time I was just on the point of starting this letter to you. And that's that (*Tatler*).[1]

I meant to tell you yesterday that we did not see Paul in town. Wonder if he came up after all — after all what? After all the drink he had on Sunday night of course. What the hosts of Enniskillen require is quart measures. Glasses as they are at present are not nearly large enough to enable them give proper demonstration of their hospitality.

Hope you're very well again and that you haven't even thought of crying. You needn't really you know. Must send you some papers today if I can. By the bye you could get the *Daily Mail* in Granard same time as the *Independent* and *Freeman* by ordering.

Slán leat. Hope I shall get a letter from you today. Are you lonely?

Fondest love,
Mícheál.

1. The magazine had apparently picked up one of Collins's forms of emphasis.

Letter 42

Mícheál, 15 Cadogan Gardens, London, to Kitty, 10 November 1921.

Kitty dearest,

This is the third letter I have written without a word from you. It's early yet of course, but I have to be at a conference at 10.30 and there's much to be done before we leave. You did not write on Monday, did you? Of course I know how busy you were — that is if you got up at all, which I am rather inclined to think was what actually happened. I wonder!

No excitement of any kind yesterday — just one meeting, but several interviews and I was late enough going to bed, I regret to say. However so long as one sticks to early rising one can't go very far wrong.

Very unpleasant days these days are. Fog gradually develops during the day. The mornings are clear enough, but the clearness quickly departs. It's doing it now and I shall want the electric light in a few minutes.

Now I must go to breakfast, and if I don't work anything more today you'll understand that it's because circumstances will be against me.

Am just able to finish it — that's all.

Fondest love,
Mícheál.

Letter 43

Mícheál, London, to Kitty, 11 November 1921.

Kitty dearest,

Yesterday evening I received your very delightful letter of Tuesday and later in the night I received your other note. That, too, was very nice. Am just scribbling a very hurried note — am going across tonight but I can't possibly get away from Dublin for the week-end. I wonder if you could come up on Saturday night — perhaps you'd wire me. Can't possibly write another word.

Fondest love,
Mícheál.

Letter 44

Mícheál, Gresham Hotel, Dublin, to Kitty, 13 November 1921.

Kitty darling,

Very sorry you were not able to travel. It was out of

the question for me to go down as I have a series of very important meetings today. It's very, very sad. I suppose you are more or less alone or have you gone to Belfast — perhaps you have. It's lucky for these people who can get away, isn't it? Gearóid has gone there.

Am just scribbling this note very hurriedly — had a Turkish bath early in the morning, then breakfast, and now this before going to my first meeting. Will try to write you a proper letter tomorrow. You'll excuse this class of production, but in the circumstances you'll understand.

Fondest love,
Mícheál.

Letter 45

Mícheál, 15 Cadogan Gardens, London, to Kitty, 15 November 1921.

Kit dearest,

This morning on my return I found your three letters awaiting me. They were very welcome indeed after my journey back, and instead of going to bed, of course I read them and I've read them more than once. They were very nice and it was just lovely of you to do that double one on Thursday. If I wrote to you in the same way you'd say I did it because I had nothing else to do. Alone, sad etc. — *that's that* — most very distinctly. Why — oh why — is that reproach of yours running through them all? You should not even give your mind to those fancies. If one broods over a thing one is very likely to give it an importance it doesn't deserve, and a doubt cultivated is apt to flourish exceedingly. Please please do put them out of your mind.

You know I was called back specially from Ireland last night — I had nearly wired you asking you to come up on the night train. Lucky I didn't for I'd have had to come in any case and then you'd have found fault — now wouldn't you? And you'd have said I could have stayed if I had liked, and I know you'll be saying I could write you a long letter today if I liked. But I couldn't — Mr G[1] is waiting for me and so will the other G[2] but I do hope to write at great length in the morning, and reply to all your *points*. One thing about H — what you call storming is just what I called 'unfair' — and it is so, if I am right. He tried to get every advocate — tried to show that it was so, whether it was or not. I feel sometimes like saying a strange thing about it — tell you sometime what it is. Of no importance though.

Hope you got the *Tatler* and *Sketch* and that they weren't very late. And here's a thing — the *Tatler* asked me to give them a sitting. What do you think of that now?

Was very glad of all your letters — but I'm sorry, very, that you think or feel I'm cold. It is not that, and I'm sure you don't think it is — not really.

Goodbye for today. I'd write you several times if I could — but you won't realise what I have on hand.

With all my love,
M.

1. Arthur Griffith.
2. Lloyd George.

Letter 46

Mícheál, London, to Kitty, 16 November 1921.

My dearest Kit,

Here I am away at the present moment from a meeting of the Delegation to telephone to someone and to write a line to you. Up very late last night and in a ferment of haste and worry all the day — I went down to my sister's place late last night — after 12 — and I found your lovely little note. I did love it. But I was sorry also for I somehow had a kind of idea that if I had been able to go to Granard, it would have been entirely to ourselves — but there you are — I was there in a way at all events. Pen bad also.

Goodbye my dear Kit,
Fondest love,
Mícheál.

Letter 47

Mícheál, London, to Kitty, 16 November 1921.

Kitty dearest,

Am just sitting down at 4 o'clock to write you a line. I have been up since 6 this morning, and this is the first moment I've got, and this will only be a moment I fear. You will not misunderstand my short notes — you won't please, will you?

By the way I sat today for my portrait — my interesting life! Absolute torture as I was expected to keep still and this, as you know, is a thing I cannot do. Another thing, the *Tatler* has asked me to give them a sitting for a photograph — and *that's that.*

Sir John Lavery is painting me.[1] Will probably get photos of the painting, so I'll send you one.

My present arrangement is to go home on Friday night — if I do, will you come to town on Saturday night? I may have to return on Sunday as we're getting into the heart of things now and I don't suppose we shall be here much longer.

How are you? I got no letter today. I suppose you are growing tired of my short ones, but if you only saw the life I have to put in you would not be surprised, and you would not blame me. You ask me what I do with the night — well I haven't been to a show since and I don't think I've been a single hour away from work. And here's a phone message and I'm just going to finish. I hope I shall hear from you tonight, but you haven't written since Friday — you haven't been busy all the time.

Goodbye dear dear K with fondest love,

Your
Mícheál.

---

1. Unlike Lavery, Leo Whelan, when he painted Collins in 1922 for the composite picture of the General Headquarters Staff of the IRA that is now in the Municipal Gallery in Dublin, declared that he was the worst sitter he ever had. 'He could not manage a moment's quiet. He was forever twisting and turning in the chair and was liable to dash from the studio without warning to attend to urgent business'. This, I fear, is reflected in the painting.

Letter 48

Mícheál, London, to Kitty, 23 November 1921.

Kitty dearest,

I'm starting this at any rate before any one has a chance of disturbing me — have just returned from Mass and nobody's up yet except the maids so that gives me an opportunity. Yet the courier has arrived from Ireland, but the despatches must wait until after breakfast.

It sounds rather queer, but I very nearly started this letter last night. Was alone in the house working until 10 or a little after it, and I thought of making sure of today's letter but somehow it seemed rather an incongruous thing to do, so I went to the Court Theatre to meet my sister and the Duggans coming out. That was my excitement for the evening! They were at *Heartbreak House* by Bernard Shaw. It's at the Court Theatre just beside here. Good, they tell me. I saw a bit of the end of it.

Endeavoured to resume immediately after breakfast and was not successful so it looks now as if I'll have to leave it until after lunch. I am being called to Hans Place for a meeting prior to going to the other fellows.

And now I have returned from the Conference and accordingly start again. Also after I had written the above I have received your letter dated from the Gresham.

10.30 evening

Somehow I had an idea that you wouldn't go home on Monday. Very accommodating those dressmakers. What did you do on Monday night? If George[1] says he's so busy, don't you believe him — he's only dodging you. I'm the only one who is busy *when I say I am.*

I do hope I shall have a chance of going to Granard on Sunday but I'll let you know. Failing that, I'd hope so much that you'll come up.

> Goodbye,
> Fondest love,
> Mícheál.

1. George was Gearóid O'Sullivan's *non de guerre*. It had done service throughout the War of Independence, and it is interesting to see Collins still using it occasionally.

Letter 49

Mícheál, London, to Kitty, 24 November 1921.

Kitty dearest,

As I am writing this there is a possibility of my going home tonight but I shall not be certain of this until after post time. However if that occurs I'll write you from Dublin or wire. But if it does occur I'll have to return perhaps on Saturday night.

We have been at it in most serious fashion all today and I'm just rushing to catch post.

Walter Cole[1] is here. He has been congratulating me about something. What do you think of that now? Goodbye Kit dear.

Fondest love,
Mícheál.

1. One of the early Sinn Féiners, and a close friend of Arthur Griffith's. Private sessions of the Dáil were often held in his house on Mountjoy Square.

Letter 50

Mícheál, London, to Kitty, November 1921.

[First page missing]

... position is very serious and I may be returning with anything but satisfactory news. However things don't look quite so desolate this morning.

How are you since? Have you gone home and are you well? Were you killed? Did Miss MacDermott[1] weep for you? And Mrs O'Connor?[2] How did you get on after you left me on Friday night? Positively I didn't get time to think — Had to work all the way on the boat. Nice crossing otherwise though. Was worried with people ...

[next page missing]

... when you were not too pleased with me. Isn't that so?

Do you want to see me? If things go according to plan I shall see you on Saturday for *two days*. May God bless you.

All my love,
Mícheál.

1. Miss McDermott was the manageress of the Grand Hotel, Greystones; see also Letter 182 (2).
2. Mrs O'Connor — was this the wife of Batt O'Connor, the builder who provided Collins with hide-outs for himself and for the gold proceeds of the Dáil Loan? Collins was a frequent visitor to the O'Connor home on Brendan Road, Donnybrook.

Letter 51

Mícheál, Wicklow Hotel, Dublin, to Kitty, 25 November 1921.

Kitty dearest,

I arrived here this morning and I do hope I shall get away tomorrow night to Granard but things are most awfully uncertain and it's quite on the cards that I may have to return to London, but I can't say yet. I'll send you a wire tomorrow either to say something definite about travelling or to tell you when I have to get away.

How are you? You deserve my silence as you've only written once during the week. I mean, I've only got one letter. Goodbye, in great haste,

Fondest love,
Mícheál.

Letter 52

Mícheál, Dublin, to Kitty, 28 November 1921.

Kitty dearest,

We got back safely — an uneventful journey. Got some hot milk at Maynooth. Badly wanted. It's a mistake to start a journey without taking something hot these days. Of course there is nothing to be said except that as usual after those visits, I am inclined to be very sorrowful, and very severe on myself, but I can't help it now. I'm greatly afraid you see the worst side of me. That alas! is a characteristic of mine. I have explained it to you often though, so you'll know what it is.

Curious thing happened today — just after Pat McCrea[1] left us, he was 'run in' for furious driving. Probably out by this time. I visited him in College St Police Station. Very funny.

Hope you won't be too busy today — that you will find time — to write a line! When did you get up? Were you more or less tired than you were yesterday? Less, I do trust.

Don't know yet whether I'm really returning tonight but I suppose I shall have to.

> Goodbye dear,
> Fondest love,
> Mícheál.

1. See Letter No. 34. Pat McCrea was a member of the famous 'Squad' that Collins linked to his intelligence staff during the Tan war; he drove an armoured car, captured from the British, into Mountjoy Gaol in an attempted rescue of Seán MacEoin.

Letter 53

Mícheál, London, to Kitty, 30 November 1921.

Kitty dearest,

I read over all your letters again last night and I started writing to you sitting up in bed but I had to give it up. Positively I was too worn out to write legibly. It was much worse than the production I turned out one night very late in Dublin. Do you recall that one? Even so I was up at 7.30 and am feeling as well and as vigorous as it is possible to feel. Don't worry about my rest. It's really all right. You know my maxim: 'It's better to wear out than to rust out'. That's really the important essential point, isn't it? Am writing this early before any one has started here. I went to St Mary's, lit a candle for you, came back, had breakfast and started this before 9! What do you think of that?

Here's a thing! I really and truly loved that suit of yours, but I was not in just the proper form on Sunday night to express my liking for it or indeed to appreciate it fully. I'd like you to know this. Do you like it? I mean this note.

Believe me I can understand your feelings about that week end, and I know how miserable the stress of my appointments must make the time for you. But how can I help it? I didn't have a minute more than you know of. If you can realise this, what does it matter if people do make suggestions like you say they did? I don't find it very agreeable sometimes, I assure you, and I don't find the forced absence very pleasant, but then it has to be seen through.

You scarcely understand my way of thinking and of doing things. I am not demonstrative (expect [*sic*] in showing my temper sometimes) and I hate demonstrative indications of feeling — I mean before people. They stand somehow in my mind for a kind of insincerity. That always makes me say that 'm'yes' of mine when I hear people at it. It may not be a pleasant way and it may not appeal to people, but there you are. It's there and I'm afraid there it will remain. It really means that I'm on the side of those who do things, not on the side of those who say things. And that's that!

That's enough, I think. You won't find this letter interesting, I'm greatly afraid, but I'm in a very troubled state of mind this morning. Troubled about many things. About you among them — first among them in my own personal mind. Do you grasp that? I'd never forgive myself if I made your life unhappy. Little wrongs I may have done people never cease coming back to my mind, let alone a matter of that kind. This is a side that perhaps you could not regard as being there, but it is there.

I was expecting a letter last night. Called to my sister's place. Nothing there. However I don't intend putting the two day rule into operation until tomorrow (*at earliest*).

Slán leat for today,
Fondest love,
Mícheál.

The delegation returned to London, and on Sunday, 4 December, Griffith, Barton and Gavan Duffy saw Lloyd George and other members of the British delegation. Collins did not join them: he was said to be 'fed up' with the muddle he had witnessed in the Dublin cabinet the day before. Under pressure from Griffith, however, he had a heart-to-heart talk with the British Prime Minister on the morning of Monday the 5th and found him ready to make concessions on the issues of an oath of allegiance, defence and trade, provided that the clauses retaining what was to be known as the Irish Free State within the Commonwealth were accepted. That, by implication, Collins agreed to. He returned at three in the afternoon with Griffith and Barton and, after a marathon session, in which further adjustments were made, the end was reached. Griffith indicated his willingness to sign the Treaty document and to recommend it to Dáil Éireann for acceptance. Collins and Duggan did so later and, later still, Barton and Gavan Duffy signed. It was then the early hours of 6 December 1921.

During these tremendous days the romance continued as if nothing else mattered. At least that is the impression one gets from Kitty's letters, but, in fairness to her, it must be said that, like the rest of the Irish world, she was following intently the press reports of what was taking place in London.

Letter 54

Mícheál, London, to Kitty, 1 December 1921.

My dear Kitty,

Ever so many thanks for your letter of Monday night — it reached me after I had posted mine, written yesterday morning. It was a very nice letter. I liked it well.

Please don't think of my cold. With very occasional exceptions there 'aint no such thing'. Above all don't think of remedies — they're no good to me as I always forget to use them or, as for instance during the past two or three years, the remedy was always somewhere else. Many a time the estimable qualities of Thermogen Wool have been dilated upon to me but I have always withstood the lure. In this present instance, however, I assure you that it's not necessary and you wouldn't in such circumstances subject me to it, would you?

Need I say there is no reason to apologise about the comfort of the week-end. Whatever other faults I may have the fault of wishing for personal comfort is not among them. And indeed this is no tribute to myself for I rather enjoy the state that people would regard as non-comfortable; therefore, its absence is pleasing enough to me. Do you understand the attitude? But comfort or not, room or not, I am looking forward to the next week-end. I greatly fear it will not be this coming one as if I'm in Dublin at all it would only mean the bare day and, therefore, out of the question for me to go down. It would not be worth your while to come up either — and you will not misunderstand this — it would only mean another Sunday week!

You'll excuse me but I do not understand your remark that you feel puzzled when you meet the elusive Michael Collins sometimes. What's it about? Do tell me.

It was a great shame that you did not waken me on Sunday night. It was what I call lack of confidence and consequently I didn't like it. Am very sorry that you didn't sleep. But you shouldn't be doing silly things when they're not necessary.

Goodbye my own dear Kitty,

With fondest love,
Mícheál.

Letter 55

Kitty to Mícheál, Wednesday night [30 November], received 2 December 1921.

My dear Mícheál,

Don't think me very spiteful to start [this] letter with 'my dear'. If I wasn't very fond of you it would be easier to write 'my darling'. But you know by this time how anxious I am to secure your love really well, and how I long for this more than anything else, so much so that it must bore you sometimes. With me nothing seems to matter except that love between the two of us. In my opinion what else matters? And there the tragedy lies. I must try and be more matter of fact and sensible in future and I'll see how it works with you. As you know by now, no matter what happens or what you could give me, I want your love more than anything else. (It's not fair to myself to write this letter *just* now, as I've just returned from Vi[1] who gave me *one* glass of wine and I suppose you would say I'm drunk! Anyway I tell you *what I had* and you can think as you wish!) It didn't take the glass of wine to write, but it makes me more silly, I suppose, and, as you say, that's that.

Delighted with your note today. I'm not so unreasonable. If you are busy, I am glad to get a *note*. You ask if I'm glad or sorry for Sunday night. Well, I'm both. You know my feelings by this time. But *do* please forgive me if I doubt you sometimes. Perhaps it is that I'm selfish, and expect too much attention. I never get tired of you, but it keeps coming up *that you are* [tired of me] and there's the trouble. It is all so selfish and so childish of me to want you so much, and not to be more practical, and one is happier when one doesn't let one's heart run away with one's head. No fear that you shall ever do that. I'll probably change and just be not so silly, and that should end all our rows. Really I wouldn't mind those rows only they are really so serious. It is too bad that our little romance should have such ups and downs.

Sweetheart, wouldn't you like me to be more sensible and not be silly? If you just tell me I shall try not to notice anything. Won't we be happy? We will, I'm sure, if you are sure. I love to hear you say *it*. Perhaps that's the whole secret. I do not hear you say it often enough. I love you to tell me all the time — I want to make you as silly as myself! I'd love you all the more. Just you and I. Nobody will know. Won't you be your real self with me. I am always with you. Ah, do please, and don't ever think by not telling me that you make me keener. Quite the reverse with me. Would you prefer I didn't tell you? But I think really that love is a thing so real and so really wonderful that, when it comes, it just makes all life different, so much so that I'm afraid to believe we are the lucky ones that can say that God gave us the biggest thing of all in life. Without it, in this awful world of uncertainty, there must be a want. Whereas it's so good to know that you have someone who won't forget you. Your trouble is her's. One not complete in anything without the other. That's my conception of love, and you are the first who made me believe in love, and that's why I wouldn't like to be ever disappointed in you. You will forgive me for saying this, won't you?

Now good bye for the present. I'd like you to burn this when finished. It's an awful production, writing it on my knee (no need to remark!) as you can guess.

Hope you are sleeping and feeling well and very happy.
I won't forget you even for one hour.

Yours with love,
Kit.

1. Violet Davis.

Letter 56

Kitty to Mícheál, received 4 December 1921 but apparently written on 1st.

My very dear Mícheál,

When I awoke this morning, the first thing I thought of was the letter I wrote last night. It was still lying on the table. It was a silly letter I know, but I decided to post it (11 o'clock post) as I have never been sorry for anything I wrote to you, no matter how silly and stupid it appeared afterwards. I was doubly glad today, when your long letter came, that I had sent it. I liked your letter very much and it made me full of resolutions. I really probably misunderstood you. You asked me if I recalled the letter you wrote one night very late in Dublin. You might not ask. I recall only too well all our little episodes before you went to London.

The connection with Dublin and you I look back on with the greatest happiness, and I delight to think about it. I 'seem' to have had no worries then, no thought of anything, but just lived for the day. Perhaps it was that I had not the same feelings for you then as I have now. (I hope you were not hinting at me in your letter when you remarked that you don't like demonstrative people . I quite agree, and hate it in public, and sometimes you must get fed up with me telling you about the change I feel so keenly that has come over me. When I cease to be surprised shortly it should be more comfortable for you. But you will forgive me just once more for boring you about it.) Then I was easily pleased and quite happy. I felt you liked me, that you were sure about it, and I didn't worry, and very sensible too. But I found that I grew to love you more and more each day, and then the worries began. I thought if you discovered this you might cool off and I tried to be a bit elusive, but then it became too serious, far too serious to my mind to hide it, and I let you know 'in every way'. But all the same I wasn't brave enough. I was afraid. Every day the feeling grew stronger and with it the fear, because I had always a feeling that if I ever thought anyone wants it, I'd be very very keen, not realising at first that you might be the one (poor you). It came on gradually (ah, you did it, 'you knew the way'! like the song). Anyhow I then realised how serious it was for both of us and, of course, I got all the more anxious to make you happy. But I had also the feeling that I wanted you to be free absolutely to change if you wished, and that's why, and I'm sure you may have misunderstood me often. I gave you so many chances just because I liked you. Otherwise I wouldn't have worried and I assure you it would have been all the same to me — as all men were alike more or less, I believed — and I could have made it easy by not saying anything, almost taking it all for granted as so many do, only you were so sincere and straight. I wanted to be the same and give you every chance. In the beginning in Dublin those ideas never entered my head seriously, although I used to talk. It was later when I realised. I fought it successfully for a short time, then I decided, if it is a question of marriage (two nights before Helen's wedding on the stairs and the night following it, when you really wanted me) why not marry the one I really love, and what a cowardly thing of me to be afraid to marry the one I really want, and who loves me just as well as any of the others I had thought of marrying.

Then London came. I should not have gone. It gave rise to such talk. People got to know about it, and I thought it better from a girl's very conventional and narrow point of view that we better have something definite, and so we have drifted. *Please*, sweetheart, *don't* misunderstand me now. I can't explain. It is only I felt, if we were ever to part, it would be easier for us both, especially for me, to do it soon, because later it would be bitter for me. But I'd love you just the same, even if we both *or you* decided on it.

Now don't think by this that I want a row or want you to end it. Not likely. I want you only not to think bad of me when we had those scenes. Testing you! With the feeling as a girl — 'better have it now than later'. If you were *me* you

68

would see it clearly too. Don't think I want you to decide definitely now. I am happy to drift and drift as long as I know you love me and we will be one day together. I fancy sometimes — as girls do — a little nest, you and I, two comfy chairs, a fire, and two books (now I'm not too ambitious) and no worries. You feeling perfectly free, as if not married, and I likewise. I do believe, as you *used* to say 'it will be a great arrangement'. I will promise you when we feel perfectly confident — as I have done for ages — 'I'll have no more rows. Truly if I didn't love you so well I wouldn't want your love so badly. I always picture — do you like my picture? — myself sitting on your knee — not the two big chairs so often — until I tire you. Cruel isn't it? We will, won't we, be real lovers? Say we will. You don't trust me or answer my important questions. And as the one I have a dim recollection of, if you liked me to love you so much or if it was a nonsense, can't you tell me all your worries? If you can't have me as a friend [who is] ready to do anything for you (almost?), who could you trust?

This must finish now and it's some letter. You couldn't bring yourself to write this sort of thing, the famous M.C. All I wish now is that it pleases you, gives you some sunshine, and helps to make the day easy for you. That will always be my ambition. With that we should have no worry.

Believe me, your own little pet, friend and everything,
Kit.

I have heaps more to write, but the post goes now. Excuse writing. In haste.
K.

Letter 57

Kitty to Mícheál, Thursday night [1 December], received 3 December 1921.

My dear sweetheart,

In the rush finishing my letter so as to have it in time for the post, I overlooked a few important things. First, only yesterday I suddenly realised that Christmas was so near

69

and I want to tell you — if there is any necessity — how I would love to have you here. All I regret now is the past Christmasses that I remember in the hotel (when it wasn't possible to have more happiness and real sport than we had, with Tom[1] and Paul and a few others) that you were absent. I know you would have enjoyed them. The hotel all to ourselves, we just went mad. This time it may be dull, but it will be more restful for you and that's what you need most after all your exciting times and strain over there. I'll be charmed if you are near me, of course. But if you would prefer to go elsewhere I'll understand. Your home crowd mightn't understand you not going back, but their loss will be my gain if you come here. I'll be glad looking forward to seeing you soon.

Hope you liked the brushes, when they were from me. Sorry you didn't have them long ago. It was a mix-up. Will finish this letter to-morrow. I'm off to bed. Nighty nighty. Pyjama Pyjama.

Friday morning

I've just got your letter and, strange to say, I knew by the whole tone of it that you weren't coming. (It was so nice!) You will have some post waiting you when you get back. I wrote you a lovely letter yesterday — today's post. This was to be the finish of it. When you get them, read the right one first. Don't forget. Otherwise you'll get mixed up. And I hope you will like them. As usual the irony. I had planned such a nice time for you *this* time, just to show you I could be nice. I was going to be just lovely to you, and give you a big kiss when you arrived, and, no matter what you said to me, not get vexed. Some strain! You would not know me. No matter how tired I was, I was not going to tell, and so you would sincerely have enjoyed it. I'll look forward to next week-end. In the meanwhile I hope you will be in the best of form.

Now about last week-end — I never told you, you would laugh — it just shows you the kind of child I am — I was jealous that Dodie[2] had your three coming home and looked at her face to see if she could tell me anything. When she got in she just said, 'I had the loan of *his* knee.' So of course

70

I smiled, and said something very nice, but felt very different. I was anxious to give you a welcome kiss, but somehow couldn't. You'd never believe I'm shy?

Did you get the brushes? They were sent on Thursday to London, as I thought perhaps you might not be crossing this week-end. It is unfortunate that you miss my lovely letters, nicer than you could ever write! Some challenge.

Now, good-bye, dear. It does seem a long long way till next week-end. Le grádh,[3]

Kit.

1. Tom Magee, Chrys's 'intended'.
2. Dodie Coyle of Enniskillen who married Fintan Murphy, a 1916 man who, at one period, was Quartermaster-General of the Volunteers.
3. With love.

Letter 58

Mícheál, 10 Downing Street, Whitehall, S.W.1. (headed paper) to Kitty, Friday, 3 December 1921, at 7 p.m. and later at Mansion House, Dublin.

Dearest Kitty,

Will you please look at the address.[1] I am actually writing here — just waiting while some of the secretaries are agreeing on a report. I have had a most awful day — conferring all the time and I am preparing to clear off now for Euston where I hope to post this.

Why haven't you written? Last letter I got from you was dated on Monday — nothing since and of course I am all impatience — are you trying for this result? If you are then you've got it. I expect I shall return on Saturday night but that is not certain and if I don't I'll send you a wire tomorrow. The probability, however, is that I must come back for a meeting.

Mansion House

I did not get away from D. St in time to post this last night, so I'm closing it here. Will send you a wire during the day, and will, if at all possible, write before I return.

With fondest love,
M.

We were 8½ hours crossing. Ran down a boat and had to put back. Killed three men.

Got the two letters last night just prior to departure. Very nice, very very nice.

M.

1. 10 Downing Street, Whitehall, London S.W.1.

Letter 59

Mícheál, 15 Cadogan Gardens, London, to Kitty, 4 December 1921.

Kitty dearest,

Got back safely this morning. No inadvertence this journey. Look at the enclosed.[1] There wasn't really any excitement at all after a few minutes.

I told you in a note posted yesterday in Dublin that I had received your Wednesday letters in London late on Friday evening — long one was ever so nice, but it was not as nice as the letter of Thursday night received by Gearóid and given to me at lunch time yesterday — you understand that I only reached Dublin at 10.30 instead of 5.30 and had to go straight to our meeting. I sent you a telegram but otherwise there wasn't a moment to do anything. We didn't even have time to have tea before we left Dublin. We had dinner on the boat, however, and didn't do at all badly. Then a sleep on the train, and am feeling in great form now.

I dislike this place intensely on a Sunday; everything so quiet, and still, and so drearily dull. The outlook now is not inviting — through smoky, grimy windows, to a drab Square. Very very unpleasant indeed — different from our own places, but then there's a job to be done, and for the moment here is the place. And *that's that.*

I am really very very grateful for your Xmas invitations. Who else will you have? I won't promise yet as I see my brother[2] has been released, and he has no one at all now and no place so that I must go to see him but this does not necessarily mean Xmas. So will only have to leave it like that for the time being. With the help of Goodness I'll see you next week end, if indeed we are going to have any

72

more free week ends at all, but then again we may. Isn't
it a pity the Hotel won't be ready? What would you like for
Xmas?

The brushes have probably turned up by this time, but
I haven't seen my sister this morning yet — it was to her place
you sent them, wasn't it?

M'yes — that was it, was it? I mean the 'loan of his knee' —
Queer, that was a thing that never struck me but that was
because of my utter faultlessness in that regard. What do
you think of that? But wouldn't it be putting too great and
too unfair a task on yourself not to be cross with me for
anything? I hope and pray you'll never have cause to be cross
with me for some things again, but it would be difficult
not to pull me up for some of [my] unpleasant ways (temper,
surliness, and so on — isn't that right?)

No. I do not take up that challenge about the letters.
That privilege I shall claim — the privilege of getting you
to imply all the nice things that are not definitely mentioned
in my letters. Will you do that and the nice way things
stand at the present moment will be made doubly nice.

Am going to a meeting now and there will be a conference
afterwards — that's my Sunday here. Don't you pity me for
my good time in London? They have just 'phoned from Hans
Place that they want me, so goodbye for the day and fondest
love,

Mícheál.

1. An extract from a newspaper, probably.
2. John or Johnny Collins, who had been interned on Spike Island.

Letter 60

*Mícheál, London, to Kitty, Monday and Tuesday, 5 and 6
December 1921.*

Dearest Kit,

Your letter of the 1st December was given to me yesterday
afternoon (soon after I had written my letter to you). I
liked it and believe me I liked it not a bit less for the thought-
fulness. If the question were of no interest at all to me

surely I could not blame you for having concern for your own future and your lifelong happiness. When it does so very closely concern myself I cannot blame you more. This is really my straightforward genuine point of view, and remember that if you ever express doubts I always have that in the back of my mind or indeed very much in the front of my mind. And that's that. When you know I think of it in this way don't you feel it gets rid of any necessity to answer your questions in detail? Tell me this.

Ever so many thanks for the brushes. They are very delightful and I do really and truly appreciate them. Míceál[1] not Míceal. I must try having this put right. No doubt it can be done.

Tuesday 6 December 1921.

Thus far had I got yesterday morning when I was called to go to a conference and what a day I had afterwards. Finished up at Downing St at 2.15 this morning. To bed about 5, and up to go to Mass and didn't (need I say it) forget your candle. My plans in regard to home are as yet uncertain. I don't know how things will go now but with God's help we have brought peace to this land of ours — a peace which will end this old strife of ours for ever.

I should have liked very much to write fully to you but today is worse than yesterday: there are all sorts of interviews, photographers etc., etc. There are further meetings to be attended also and therefore I must finish. You will not think any worse of me by not receiving a letter this morning — you will see I wrote part of it, so that the spirit was there all right.

Every blessing to you
and Fondest love,
M.

1. From this on, Kitty consistently used this form in the Gaelic script. We have used the Roman form, to avoid a dotted c.

Letter 61

Mícheál, London, to Kitty, 7 December 1921.

My dearest Kit,

My letters have got all upside down — indeed I am afraid that mine of yesterday was not posted until late in the evening — too late I fear for the post but perhaps not. I did not return to Ireland last night but am going tonight and if at all possible I'll come along to see you on Saturday or Sunday, but please don't take anything as being certain at present. I look forward now to a busier time than ever and the immediate future is so uncertain that it would be entirely unsafe to venture on any definite arrangements. However I'll do my very best to let you know. You won't mind if my letters get somewhat uncertain for a time, but I will really do my best to avoid this too.

I shall write you again today if I get a chance, but I am finishing this so that there may be no mistake about your getting something from me.

Fondest love,
Mícheál.

Collins and Griffith reached Dublin on Thursday morning, 8 December, and had some reason to expect that de Valera would support the settlement to which they had put their signatures recognising that it was the best settlement of a Dominion character, to which they all were understood to be committed, that could be achieved in the circumstances. But the previous night, when Griffith's personal secretary Kathleen McKenna, reached Dublin she found Gearóid O'Sullivan 'black in the face and whistling between his teeth in that annoying fashion of his. He said "The fat's in the fire. The so-and-so (de Valera) and his so-and-so buddies (Brugha and Stack) won't accept what Mick has signed; the country will be quartered; nothing can prevent a split in the army and civil war."' Collins, of course, was under no illusion as to the limitations of the Treaty seen from a republican angle, but he was to insist that, if it did not give all that he wanted, it provided the means to secure it; and Griffith declared that it had no more finality than that they were the last generation on the face of the earth. De Valera's rejection was negatived in the Dáil cabinet by one vote, and the Dáil began a debate which ended with the Treaty being approved by seven votes. Long before then, Kitty had become a solid Treaty supporter and advocate.

Letter 62

Kitty to Mícheál, Saturday, received Sunday 12 December 1921.

My very dear Mícheál,

Both your little notes which arrived on first post today were a lovely surprise.

Please don't worry. All will be well. Opinion is *just* the same. Seán C.[1] is here just now. He says he's urging ratification ever since the Treaty, and if the Treaty is not ratified [by the Dáil] the country will ratify. 90 to 95 per cent of Connacht are in favour of ratification. He says that he'll enclose a note. So that's all right.

I was wondering if perhaps you sent a wire today, as the wires are cut here. None going or coming.

Don't thank me for praying. I'd do more than that for you; in fact I'd only love the chance of helping you in anything. Would love to be a necessity to you in some way. I mean I love to feel you wanted me always *beside* you, just the way Daddy and Mother used to be, but I feel I'm no use.

We expect Paul tonight. Hope you will try and rest and sleep, and do all or some of the things I suggested, egg flips etc. You do need them. When are you going to have a rest and get away from it all, until I have you all to myself as you know I always suggested? Nothing queer [in that] ! Only I think it would be lovely and peaceful. God is good and we hope for the best.

My love and a kiss,
from your own,
Kit.

1. Not identified.

Letter 63

Kitty to Mícheál — a fragment of a letter written possibly in December 1921.

. . . Some of these people have put their foot in it and want to try and get out of it but — as you would say — 'that's not my fault!'

All will end well. Ireland knows only too well that you are her strong friend, and the people are not fools. I haven't to explain anything. They grasp the whole thing all right.

I send you my love and a great big hug, and several kisses and when you are inclined to get annoyed, just think of my kisses (some conceit!) and how I love you and think you are so good and brave and wonderful. But I'd better not spoil you and have to pay the penalty!

I am getting quite daring in the things I say to you. I meant to be so reserved and leave you guessing as to what I really thought. You will soon know it all, and then. . . .

Bye bye, Good luck to you and all from
                         Kit.

I had a nice letter from Mrs Leigh-Doyle[1] yesterday.

1. The Leigh-Doyles, who had houses in Carlow and the Rathgar suburb of Dublin, were good friends of Collins, and provided him with one of his Dublin hideouts.

The Treaty had to run the gauntlet in the Palace of Westminster as well as in Dáil Éireann; and a couple of letters which Collins passed to Kitty — they are among her letters, anyway — show Lady Hazel Lavery's concern that the Irish commitments of the British coalition government should be endorsed by the Lords and Commons. The Belfast-born portrait painter Sir John Lavery and his young and beautiful American wife had opened their house at Kensington to the Irish delegation and made many useful contacts for them. They had a great regard for Collins and strove to promote the interests of the Irish delegation, but in order to protect his name and to assure Kitty that there was nothing in the stories that she might be hearing about Lady Lavery's association with him, he sent these letters to Granard. It will be noted later that, for a similar reason he advised Kitty, when coming to see him in the Gresham Hotel in Dublin, not to come alone.

Letter 64

Lady Hazel Lavery, 5 Cromwell Place, London S.W. to Collins, probably 10 December 1921.

My dear Michael,

Your kind letter came swiftly to my comfort, and I cannot thank you enough for your thought for me in the midst of all that furious pressure of work! So much more important than the 'Lost Letter of a Lady' — and would that not by the way make a good title for a romantic novel?

The letter *is* lost I fear and I picture the poor thing wandering desolately about like a pigeon in a storm looking for its owner Mr Michael Collins! and finally bruised and broken, pathetically rejected by man and Post Office, forced to struggle back to Hazel — admittedly a failure, and all its burden of news about perfectly unimportant personal matters having been read by indifferent eyes alas!

Yesterday I went to hear W.[1] speak. It was very long *but excellent* I thought and generally well received, excepting *of course* by the Tories who still rage, albeit more and more powerlessly.

Poor W. is worried about his little girl, the delicious small Sarah who like her parent has an acquisitive nature and has contrived to catch scarlet fever rather badly. She is the greatest darling of a child and Winston always says he thinks she must belong to me as she has red hair and I love *her* so!

To-day I lunch with Lady Fitzalan[2] and on Tuesday with the Chamberlains.[3] I have not seen L. (the other Lord we discussed the other day)[4] as after dinner (?) that night I went home I was so very tired, but I had a talk with Philip[5] about the matter. He is a clever creature, with imagination and warm towards you (you must get him that dog) also. Thanks to his oriental blood he delights in a secret and he

undoubtedly has a certain influence over his illustrious (?)
Master (?)[6]

I shall not expect an answer unless you tell a secretary
to say simply that you have received this letter so that I
shall know that it has not gone a-missing. I really mean this
sure. Irish *sure* I understand you know.

>Bless you Michael always,
>Yours,
>H.

P.S. I found this portion of a wonderful book in an old
shop. I am trying hard to get an intact copy to send you as
you would delight in it I know, and be interested in all the
facts about the French Revolution. The actual title I think
is called Madame de Sabrian and the Chevalier de Boufflers.[7]
You may have read it.

>H.L.

1. Winston Spencer Churchill, then a Liberal and Colonial Secretary in
   the coalition government led by Lloyd George.
2. The wife of the last Lord Lieutenant of Ireland.
3. Austen Chamberlain, the leader of the Conservative Party and of
   the House of Commons, had taken part in the Irish negotiations.
4. The 7th Marquess of Londonderry, a leading Northern Unionist
   politician.
5. Philip Snowden, Socialist MP since 1906 who was to become
   Chancellor of the Exchequer in the Labour and National govern-
   ments.
6. Presumably J. Ramsay MacDonald.
7. See L. Ó Broin, *The Chief Secretary*, 170.

Letter 65

*Lady Hazel Lavery, 5 Cromwell Place, London, S.W. to
Collins, n.d., probably 14 December 1921.*

My dear Michael,

I have just come from the House of Lords where the
Lord Chancellor[1] replied with his usual devastating urbanity
to the bitter but rather futile sarcasm of Carson.[2] All the
same the division was a very very close thing for the Govt:
only a majority of *one*! I saw Winston who is much concerned

over the two shootings of Lt Mead (?) and the officer in Cork with the foreign name (cannot spell it or remember) and he asked if I would please write to you and say how difficult the incident has made matters here. The old Die Hards have taken a vigorous new lease of life on it. Of course he *knows* you are doing everything you possibly can, and *I* hate to write to you and add a further weight of anxiety to your many cares. Please please forgive me.[3]

I lunched with the Austen Chamberlains to-day, and sat next to him. We talked about you and he spoke most warmly and kindly of both you and Mr Griffiths [sic] and I feel you have a true friend in him.

In the matter of Lord Londonderry I find rather dissatisfaction. Winston saw him at luncheon and had a long talk but I imagine from what I have been able to gather not an altogether successful one. Lord L. has intimated that 'he would like to see me on the subject' and I don't know exactly what that may mean. Almost anything I should think.

Meanwhile all our thoughts and prayers are with you Michael. I purchased a most expensive and gigantic candle on Sunday at early *Mass* and burnt it for your victory.

God bless you,

H.

I wrote to you last Friday. I hope it has not shared the fate of the last letter. This one I am sending through Eddie Marsh.[4]

1. The Earl of Birkenhead (F. E. Smith). Though a Conservative and Unionist he solidly supported Lloyd George during the negotiations. He also conceived a considerable regard for Collins.
2. Sir Edward Carson, the outspoken leader of the Unionist protest against home rule.
3. At a private session of the Dáil on 16 December, E. J. Duggan drew attention to the fact that, within the previous three days, six members of the British Crown forces had been shot in different parts of the country. Two were killed, at Ballybunion and near Kilmallock. He read a letter from the British asking for the repudiation of these atrocious breaches of the Truce.
4. Sir Edward Marsh, one of Churchill's secretaries.

The next run of letters may have been concerned with an announcement of their engagement. The Dáil discussion of the Treaty began on Wednesday 14 December. Mícheál had been in Granard the previous Sunday and lost his watch. The hectic pace is telling on him.

Letter 66

Mícheál, Dublin, to Kitty, 12 December 1921.

Kitty dearest,
   Am back but I'm so tired that I can scarcely remain awake. This is a line just to tell you so, and to say I am thinking very very much of you today, also to say that, no matter how short my note is, I am writing it.
   May God bless you always and may I see you soon again.

Your own,
Mícheál.

Letter 67

Mícheál, Dublin, to Kitty, 13 December 1921.

My dearest Kit,
   Yes of course you are right to some extent. Without your asking for it I had decided to do it and mean to do it. No more at the present moment.[1]
   Every thought and wish to you.

M.

1. The significance of this is not apparent. Obviously as the next letter shows, Kitty has been worrying about the matter.

Letter 68

Kitty, to Mícheál, Wednesday, received 13 December 1921.

My very dear Mícheál,
   Needn't tell you how pleased I was to-day when your note arrived to say that you have decided on what I was worrying about.[1]

I went to Mass this morning and lit three candles. Then when I came back, I had a perfect morning. I read the 'Mad Love'[2] and enjoyed it, for about an hour, and then break-fasted beside a lovely fire — it was very cold — and felt quite happy. I am sure you will be amused at this. Some day I must send you the book, and some night, if you can't sleep, you can pass an hour reading it. Rubbish, but I like the girl so far: I have only read about 40 pages. Of course, if I don't like the ending, I'll not send it. I tried not to think too much to-day because I'd worry so much. Hope you are feeling all right. We won't know anything definite yet [about your coming] until end of the week. I suppose that you are going to Cork?

Did you see Seán [Shane] Leslie's article about you yesterday? Very nice I thought.[3]

It was very good of you to write yesterday and you so busy, and I was delighted. I am just longing to see you again, and I'll be praying for you till then.

Writing in shop, so excuse my sending this to the Gresham. Hope you get it. No need to send you any more love, you have it all. Will say bye bye now. Fondest love, and the best of good luck from your own,

Kit.

1. See note to preceding letter.
2. One of seventy-seven novelettes written by Charlotte M. Brame. One can easily imagine from the title what this particular one was like.
3. Shane Leslie (1885-1971), a noted biographer and writer on religious and philosophical themes. His mother and Winston Churchill's mother were sisters. He became a Catholic in 1908, became interested in the Gaelic Revival movement, dropping the names of John Randolph he had been christened with, and espoused the nationalist cause.

Letter 69

Kitty, to Mícheál, Tuesday, received 14 December 1921.

My own sweetheart,

I don't suppose you'll have much time to read this, but I just want to tell you that I'll be praying for you that you may do and say the thing that's best for Ireland.[1]

When Paddy[2] got back last evening (7 o'c) we got him in here to hear the news. Glad you got back safely — and hope you were in time. Your letter to-day was a lovely surprise, though I half expected it. I was very sorry you missed the train. I was delighted with myself. Only I was sorry you felt so tired. I just got panicky before you left at how awful you were looking and all you had to face. So I pray you may have a rest and a sleep. I felt a bit bad during the market, but when night came I went to bed and never woke until 9 o'c! I am thinking of you all day [today] and hope you are not worrying. And don't forget me. I mean that I *do* think of you — your pal and 'everything' (What? Everything?).

I am trying hard to get your watch, but in vain so far. Where could you have dropped it? Do you want it badly, and I'll offer a reward etc. and try harder? It must have dropped on the grass or we would have heard it drop.

I am going to Mass in the morning for you. Will you go for me and yourself?

Vi. had a letter from Paul. Paddy couldn't find him. He doesn't stay at the Gresham. I hope you weren't vexed with my letter yesterday, but it worried me all day and I had to get rid of it. Don't blame me, only take my advice this time.

I was delighted to see you on Sunday. I hope you thought I looked pleased, and well. I felt awfully excited when you came. I always do, and it takes me ages to get used to you. It was lovely to see you, only you were so tired and longed to sleep. It was I kept you up in a kind of way. I mean if I ran away to bed, you might have gone — and I was sorry. But that's always the way with you and I, we never want to separate. I hope it will always be the way. But it will, won't it?

I loved your note to-day. You feel very sure *now*. Sure you might guess before you came on Sunday that I would think like you, and your worry be my worry. But you must have felt on Sunday that there was a stronger link by your remarks. It is my nature, apart from everything else, to be sympathetic, and I like people who are like this.

Hope your cold has gone. Was the drive very cold going

back? I did feel sorry for you all. My regards to Gearóid.
I'll be watching the *post* and pretending to myself that I
am not expecting a letter! Funny isn't it? When will I see
you again? My love and a big hug from your own little pet,
Kit.

P.S. In future where will I address letters? Will you get them
yourself if the Gresham is on it? I don't want to trouble
G[earóid].

1. This was the day the Dáil met in the council chamber of University
   College, Dublin, to deal with the peace treaty and Collins was naturally expected to be one of the principal speakers.
2. Paddy Cusack.

Letter 70

Mícheál, Wicklow Hotel, Dublin, to Kitty, 14 December 1921.

My dearest Kit,
    Got your letter today. Ever so many thanks. Am trying
to show you that you are in my personal mind notwithstanding
all cares and worries. I have so many. Do keep on praying
for me.
    Write to Gresham Hotel. Mark Personal. Put in inner
envelope and mark Personal only.
With all my love,
M.

Letter 71

Mícheál, Dublin, to Kitty, 15 December 1921.

Kitty dearest,
    Yours received safely. It is very good of you to pray and
write as you are doing these days. In a few days I may be
free from everything and then we can see how the future
goes. It's all a dreadful strain and it's telling a good deal on
me, but, with God's help, things will be all right and some
good will have been done in any case, and that's something.
With my fondest love,
Mícheál.

Letter 72

Kitty, to Mícheál, Thursday, received 16 December 1921.

My own sweetheart,

I am sorry to learn from your note that you are worrying.
I am so glad that you are keeping me in your mind and that
you realise I am thinking of you all the time and praying
for you. I went to Mass this morning and again this evening.
I said a little prayer in chapel when passing the church
coming from a funeral. Larry is away. So he asked me to
go. Very exciting occupation.

The papers to-day are interesting enough. It is nothing
but Collins *here*, Collins *all* the time, and as far as I can
gather from strangers coming here, it's the same all over
Ireland. Had a letter to-day from Fr Coyle; he says it's great
up there[1] and just wonderful, the terms.

You don't say you had your moustache off? I'd love to
see you.

Have just heard a man speaking about *you*, and it was just
wonderful. You wouldn't believe it. Such compliments —
your strong will, great personality etc.

I hope everything will end well and that you won't worry,
that you will be too sensible to worry about petty jealousies.

I send you everything, including myself (I mean in spirit!).

Your own,
Kitty.

1. In the North of Ireland.

Letter 73

*Mícheál, Gresham Hotel, Dublin, to Kitty, 16 December
1921.*

Kit dearest,

Your letter just received. Am up early this morning, and
am not feeling well at all unfortunately. The times are getting
worse indeed and these coming days will be worse still, but
I suppose they'll be over and done with soon enough. Am
staying in town for the week-end — at least it's not a matter

of staying in town, but of sitting through meetings all the time.

Your letter was very nice and pleasant and I do like these messages from you. I appreciate them so much that I never return them — just in the *same way* I mean of course.

Goodbye for today dearest,

> Your own,
> Mícheál.

Letter 74

Kitty, to Mícheál, Friday, received 17 December 1921.

My very dear Mícheál,

I suppose you are killed with work as well as worry. I am very lonely at the thought of not seeing you this week-end; in fact I am very lonely just now. I suppose you'll be in Dublin this week-end. It seems to me ages and ages since we met, although this week passed quietly enough.

No news in papers to-day. Is Paul still in town? He is silly to be taking — considering — one side or another. Someone here said they met him.

You must be having a very anxious time, but don't worry, all will yet be well, and it won't be your fault if the country is brought into trouble again. You did your best. The people here have no thought but *one*, and *you* are the one. After all the people about here have got some sense left.

I am A.1, only so lonely for you, and wondering when we can meet again. Lionel[1] wrote to say he may come over on Sunday. I might let him come just for the fun of things! We expect Chrys and Helen next week. I am praying for you that you may be all right and not worry. Hope you are going to bed early as I asked you to do and having lots to drink(!)[2] Don't be vexed with me, sweetheart. Where are you staying? Gresham, I expect.

It's a lovely evening here, and what would I give if we could just have a lovely little walk and a little talk the same as last Sunday night. I liked it, and it was a surprise! I was always wondering *when* you would ask me for a walk, and talk to me. So of course I was delighted. Did you enjoy it? But I'm afraid you were too worried. That's the only thing. You were not in the same form as I was, and I was sorry. Did I talk too much that night? I'll have to be a better listener. If you have a spare minute write me a line to say how you are, as I'm always thinking of you. I think what you said (on the bed) on Sunday quite true now. We have nothing to write to each other now. I feel it now (only just that anxiety to meet you). It is nice to have got to this stage I suppose.

Tell Mrs Duggan I send my regards if you see her at all. Also all the boys. Dublin must be a fairly exciting place just now. When will you be able to have a rest, I wonder. You who have required it after your experience in London, much less all that you have on hands now.

Will say bye bye, dear, with fondest love, and a dozen hugs and kisses from your own loving,

Kit.

1. See Letter 177.
2. Kitty is joking. Collins was not what one would call a drinker.

Letter 75

Mícheál, Dublin, to Kitty, Saturday, 17 December 1921.

Kit dearest,

Yes I think you might have L[1] over on Sunday (you will have had him or not by this time) as it will help you to pass a few hours. It will probably do him some good also. Poor chap!

I do feel so neglectful — yet you understand now, don't you, dear Kit? Although this letter will not reach you until Monday it will show you — I mean my writing of it this morning — that I have you before my mind in spite of everything and you will be there always.

I did indeed enjoy that walk ever so much. It was funny that you should have been thinking when I would ask you. Am glad, therefore, that you didn't have to make that advance. I would have spoiled it for you. But it is delightful to be out with you — it is so much healthier than remaining indoors.

Am as usual rushing.

With fondest love,
Mícheál.

1. This is Lionel Lyster who is also referred to in Letter 74.

There are no letters from Kitty in the collection for the rest of December and for the first few days of January 1922 though she continued to write. There are further gaps in what she wrote in January, but Mícheál's letters appear reasonably complete. The Dáil debate on the Treaty was adjourned from 22 December till 3 January.

Letter 76

Mícheál, Dublin, to Kitty, Saturday, 17 December 1921.

K. dear,

Am sending this note by hand by Seán[1] so as to send you some message for tomorrow. Am writing this very late on Saturday night, still at Dáil meeting and very worn out indeed. But am thinking of you and would dearly love to travel with Seán tonight — so as to see you, but alas I cannot do it.

Goodbye dear and God bless you.

Fondest love,
Mícheál.

1. Seán MacEoin.

Letter 77

Mícheál, Gresham Hotel, Dublin, to Kitty, 18 December 1921.

My dear Kitty,

Am taking advantage of a temporary cessation to drop you a line. By this time you will have received my 'scrag' per

88

Seán. I do hope you will go back to liking Seán as you used to.

Don't know yet what I can do for Xmas — or where I can go. In the end I shall probably stay in town. However, if I do that, I'll try to run down to Granard, for at any rate one day.

All this business is very, very sad. Harry[1] has come out strongly against us. I'm sorry for that, but I suppose that like many another episode in this business [it] must be borne also. I haven't an idea of how it will all end but, with God's help, all right. In any event I shall be satisfied. Don't know whether or not we shall finish tomorrow, but it's hardly likely. Anyhow you'll see from the papers. If anything of real interest occurs tomorrow I shall send you a wire.

No letter from you today. I wonder why?
God be with you and keep you safe for me.
Fondest love,
Mícheál.

Any account of watch? It must be in Vi's if anywhere. If not there, don't bother please. 'Bye.

1. A telegram from Harry Boland had been read at a private session of the Dáil on 15 December announcing that in his capacity as deputy for Roscommon-Mayo he desired to record his vote against the Treaty and hoped that the Dáil would reject that instrument.

Letter 78

Mícheál, Dublin, an unfinished note, to Kitty, 22 December 1921.

My own Kit,

Your letter this morning was very very nice. I think your letters do get nicer and nicer — at any rate that's what I think about them.

Now we may finish up today in this Assembly but that I don't know

Letter 79

Mícheál, Dublin, to Kitty, 23 December 1921.

My dearest Kit,

The wee note which accompanies this was written yesterday morning but the day came so strenuous that I was unable to finish it. You'd scarcely credit a thing like that, would you? Today is, however, somewhat of a free day — alas! free only from the routine of a debate — and I must try to do some shopping. What shall I get you? I must get it today as I may have to go to Cork by the night train tonight. My plans are still uncertain for Xmas (at least my personal plans) but it is practically certain that I must go to Cork. This will mean of course that I can't get down to you but I'll go down some time around New Year's day, perhaps on Friday, and I could then return on Monday, but I'll let you know this directly I return from Cork. That Donegal visit certainly looks very enticing and I am really sorry the offer could not be taken advantage of just now but it will some time D.V.

Now you may not hear from me again until I do return — it is possibly no use writing as the delays would be terrible. However I may send a wire. Am rushing away now to see A. G.[1] Bye Bye. Best of times for Xmas. Don't overeat yourself! Please give them all my regards. With all my very fondest love to you and many a special thought and wish at this time.

Yours,
M.

You needn't have been so quick with that £15. Why didn't you keep it? Love again.

M.

1. Arthur Griffith.

Letter 80

Mícheál, Gresham Hotel, Dublin, to Kitty, 28 December 1921.

My dearest Kit,

I have just received your letter and am writing a line before a meeting starts. Am looking forward to a very strenuous day as we are working hard for the resumption after Xmas.

By this time you will have seen George.[1] When he left, my intention was to go down tomorrow but I doubt very much now if I can do that as I have to attend to so many things but I'll do it if I possibly can. Failing it I'd try the 1.30 train from here on Friday — this so as to see you before going to the dance — Of course you must go to it and you know well I understand and you know well I would not (even if I was so thoughtless) in fairness ask you to stay away. Think of the way I saw you for a few moments only and how I was always getting you to suit my convenience.

I have been interrupted about ten times since I started so I must close now. Awfully glad you liked the 'things'.

Fondest love,
M.

1. See note 1 to Letter 48.

Letter 81

Mícheál, Dublin, to Kitty, 29 December 1921.

My dearest Kitty,

Am as usual — you'll say — scribbling a note to let you know that I'm thinking of you. My present intention is to go down tomorrow by the 1.30 train and I should like you to meet me with a car at Edgeworthstown. Of course if you can't come please don't worry, but you'll be able to send the car, I'm sure.

This is all until I see you. God bless you meanwhile.

Fondest love,
Mícheál.

No letter from you today.

Letter 82

Mícheál, Gresham Hotel, Dublin, to Kitty, 2 January 1922.

Kitty dearest,

Am writing a line to you to say I've got back. Just missed a lovely accident.

Bye dear dear Kit.

Mícheál.

The burden of the criticism in the resumed Dáil debate was that the Republic had been abandoned, and that it was now a case of 'Heads up into the Empire'. Accusations of bad faith filled the air. Collins and those who followed his lead were 'traitors'. There were allusions to the 'atmosphere of London', to a coalition between Downing Street and the delegation, to Collins the Fleet Street hero who was worse than Castlereagh, to the likelihood that he and Griffith had been drunk or drugged when they signed the Treaty. Madame Markievicz retailed a suggestion that Princess Mary's intended wedding to Lord Lascelles had been broken off in order that she might marry Collins who was to become the first Governor of the Irish Free State. The remark annoyed Collins when he heard it and he protested in the Dáil: 'When the deputy for a division in Dublin was speaking to-day', he said, 'she made reference to my name and to the name of a lady belonging to a foreign nation that I cannot allow to pass. Some time in our history as a nation a girl went through Ireland and was not insulted by the people of Ireland. I do not come from the class that the deputy for the Dublin division comes from; I come from the plain people of Ireland. The lady whose name was mentioned is, I understand, betrothed to some man. I know nothing of her personally, but the statement may cause her pain, and may cause pain to the lady who is betrothed to me. I just stand in that plain way, and I will not allow without challenge any deputy in the assembly of my nation to insult any lady either of this nation or of any other nation.'

He drew Kitty's attention to the matter in a note on the same day. He was to suffer much more as the debate went on and, as behind the scenes, tortuous discussions took place in an effort to avoid dividing the Dáil on the Treaty and to provide for de Valera's presidential position. These were all unsuccessful, drawing from Collins on 5 January a *cri de coeur*: 'This is the worst day I have had yet — far far the worst. May God help us all'. Harry Boland had joined his bitter critics. Outside the chamber he was friendly enough, and Mícheál was able to tell him how things stood between him and Kitty.

Letter 83

Mícheál, Gresham Hotel, Dublin, to Kitty, 3 January 1922.

Kitty dearest,

I would have posted the enclosed at the Broadstone[1] yesterday evening but I thought Maud was going and that she'd take it. However she did not go and consequently you have no letter today and I'm very, very sorry about that, but here it's for you now. And Kit dear, dear Kit, I'm so happy about it all, much much more happy as I think more and more of it all. Do you? I'm sure you do though, and I'm so contented. And that's that.

Fondest love,
Mícheál.

1. The main station in Dublin of the Midland Great Western Railway which served the Longford area.

Letter 84

Mícheál, Dublin, to Kitty, Tuesday, 3 January 1922, telegram.

My dearest Kitty,

This will reach you before the letters I sent today. My dear dear Kitty, see the reference to yourself and Princess Mary of England.

My Betrothed,
My fondest Love,
Mícheál.

Letter 85

Mícheál, Dublin, to Kitty, 5 (?) January 1922.

My own own Kitty,

Just one or two lines. This is the worst day I have had yet — far far the worst. May God help us all.

I got no letter from you. I wonder why. In awful haste.

My fondest love,
Mícheál.

How did you get on at Killashee?[1]

1. Killashee was where Alice Cooney, who was to marry Seán MacEoin, lived.

Letter 86

Mícheál, Dublin, to Kitty, 6 January 1922.

My dearest Kit,

I am truly sorry that you didn't receive a letter from me yesterday. It was not my fault as I did write a little note. Some rascal didn't post it maybe, but if that is so we'll be forgiving won't we Kit? Now with regard to the other letter, it's quite all right, I think, but I wouldn't like to change a word of it as I have a kind of hesitancy in recommending anything for that particular thing, as you know *best* yourself. I mean you know as well as I do. That is, we both know equally. Am I not getting too much like you already?

Saw H[1] last night. He was friendly, of course, and very nice. I'm afraid though he was not so nice today, but not about you — I mean not on the subject of you. I'm afraid he wasn't fair in his home coming in what he said about our side today. He's working like the very devil against us, but God is good. Must finish, my dear dear Kit. Fondest love.

Your
Mícheál.

1. Harry Boland.

94

Letter 87

Mícheál, Dublin, to Kitty, 9 January 1922.

My dearest Kitty,

I'm absolutely fagged out and worn out and everything, but I send you this note to give my little remembrance of you. If you knew how the other side is 'killing' me — God help me — We had to beat them again today. Please come up as soon as you can or I'll wire when my brother Johnny comes up. In awful haste and trying to catch a post so that you'd know I was thinking of you.

My fondest love,
Kitty dear,
Mícheál.

Letter 88

Harry Boland, Dublin, to Kitty, 10 January 1922.

Kitty,

I want to congratulate you. M.[1] told me of your engagement, and I wish you long life and happiness.

Ever yours,
H. Boland.

1. Mícheál.

Letter 89

Mícheál, Dublin, to Kitty, 11 January 1922.

Kitty dear,

Your letter came safely this morning and I was very sorry to hear that you were in bad form. I hope you've recovered after seeing today's papers. I wired you to say I would go down on the 1.30 train on Saturday. I wired because I feared you might think my depression would make it necessary to come up — not that I didn't want to see you, but to let you know everything was all right once I'd got your letter. And I hope you'll be likewise when you get mine. Yes indeed, the whole business was awful and I feel exactly like you about it. Wishing to God I could be with you and had left it all. The tactics of the opposition were not very creditable at times, but a great many things are allowable in positions like this — and that's that.

With all my love,
Mícheál.

Letter 90

Mícheál, Dublin, to Kitty, 12 January 1922

My dearest Kit,

One little thing in your letter today — I did not tell Harry — just said to him that he had little chance in *that* quarter now, so you're not to worry about that. My brother Johnny is here today and I must get you to see him somehow before he goes away this time but I'll talk to you about it when I see you — and honestly you wouldn't believe how I am looking forward to Saturday and I do hope that nothing will go wrong to keep me here.

I can't write at this damned table as everybody is shaking it and, in addition, my pen is bad so I'm in a sad way for those two reasons. And further, this place is full of people and I'm wishing to God I was away with you.

Goodbye for today, dearest Kit.

Fondest love,
Mícheál.

After the Dáil voted to approve the Treaty, on 7 January, a Provisional Irish Free State government was formed with Collins as its chairman; and on Monday 16 January the process of transferring power from the British took a mighty step.

Letter 91

Mícheál, Dublin, to Kitty, 13 January 1922.

Kitty dearest,

Your wee note received today. I was glad to get it for I had kind of feared that you might not have written in view of my visit. I wonder if you are writing today? That will be a test.

I'm looking forward very much indeed to seeing you after all the turmoil here, and to a quiet nice week-end with you. Are you feeling this way also? If anything intervenes tomorrow I shall be wild. And then, of course, there's the rail strike, so will have to motor back. Did I tell you of our last journey back? May God be with you until I see you.

Very fondest love,
Mícheál.

Letter 92

Mícheál, Dublin, to Kitty, 16 January 1922.

My dearest dearest Kitty,

I am as happy a man as there is in Ireland today. My thoughts just now are all with you, and you have every kind wish and feeling of mine. Have just taken over Dublin Castle,[1] and am writing this note while awaiting a meeting of my Provisional Government. What do you think of that? Otherwise I see all sorts of difficulties ahead, but never mind. Please come up tomorrow night — send a wire. Failing that, Wednesday. There is nobody like you, I find, and I wish I'd been nicer to you. *'Twas my fault.*

Fondest love, dear Kit,
Your own,
Mícheál.

1. Dublin Castle for centuries had been the centre of British power in Ireland, and the symbol of everything against which Irishmen revolted. Its surrender to Collins was, therefore, a supreme occasion, and it is surprising how little he makes of it.

Collins set up the headquarters of his government temporarily in the City Hall, next door to Dublin Castle. Kevin O'Higgins was to describe them in later years as 'simply eight young men standing amidst the ruins of one administration with the foundations of another not yet laid, and with wild men screaming through the keyhole!' There were many problems, that of the North immediately the most pressing. There, the talk of a Boundary Commission and the release of internees caused the Unionists to react as they always did in such a situation. They attacked the Catholic ghettoes in Belfast, killing thirty people in one night, and driving refugees in a stream across the border. In reaction IRA columns, with direction and arms surreptitiously supplied by Collins, crossed the border, seized Unionist hostages and ambushed Ulster Special Constables at Clones railway station. Collins went to London on 20 January to see Sir James Craig, the Northern Prime Minister, and Kitty saw him off on the mail boat at Dunleary, as he spells it. Agreement was reached between them on some matters and Collins called off the boycott of Belfast goods that had operated since September 1920. The basic issues remained unsolved, however, and further meetings were contemplated, the first of these in Dublin. In the South the division on the Treaty, and particularly in the ranks of the IRB and IRA, was already making life intolerable for Collins.

The sad little letter from Mrs de Valera, which strayed somehow into the Collins-Kiernan correspondence, is important. Collins had looked to Sinéad's financial needs while her husband was in America in 1919 and 1920; and the arrangements then made were apparently continued through 1921 and to the end of January 1922. Despite the 'split' on the Treaty, Sinéad's friendship for Collins did not falter.

Letter 93

Kitty, to Mícheál, Monday, received 17 January 1922.

My love,

Hope you got back safely. It was a cold morning and I'm sure the train wasn't warm. Am just beginning to feel sleepy now. All day I kept up splendidly. Got up at 10.30, 'about', and didn't feel too tired until now, so I'll be off to dreamland at, say 7 o'clock. But good resolutions, whenever I make them, don't materialize. Shall write later. So you will excuse this, written in shop. Peg and I are here alone. She was very funny about you this morning.

Hope to go up Wednesday, perhaps, and because of this I am not so lonely — but fairly bad.

Nighty, nightie. Pyjama Pyjama.

Love from your little pet,
Kit.

P.S. Had a letter this morning from Mrs Kevin O'Higgins.[1] Now be good. Go to sleep. Remember.

1. Bridie Cole, a teacher of English at Knockbeg College, Carlow, who, during the Treaty negotiations, had married Dáil Éireann's Assistant Minister for Local Government.

Letter 94

Mícheál, Dublin, to Kitty, 17 January 1922.

My own dear Kit,

Ever so many thanks for your little note received this morning. I was really delighted — and I was sorry to hear you were so tired. Are you feeling all the better of the two walks now? Really and truly, I feel very much improved for my week end. This is honestly true — even though I know I did not properly appreciate my feeling and luck while I was away. No, the train journey was not too bad. The day was sunny and the carriage was not cold. I got some very hot tea at Mullingar, and so did not do badly. Am looking forward to seeing you tomorrow. Will you wire me, or shall I take it for granted that you'll come on the evening train? I hope you won't leave it until midnight. Where are you staying? The Gresham gets worse and worse.

My fondest love, dear Kit,
Mícheál.

Letter 95

Mícheál, on night mail to London, Friday night, 20 January 1922, and in London next morning.

My dearest Kitty,

Am writing this on the train just before going to bed. I have been thinking of you all through the journey. You are somehow very vividly before my mind and very much with me just now. May it be always like this any time we have to leave each other. Will finish this letter in the morning but I wanted to write these few lines before lying down, and now I'll say a small prayer for you. Goodnight my Kit.

Just into London at the Jermyn Court Hotel — going to bed for two hours or so — then — what a day? Feeling well enough after the journey. You're asleep now I suppose — it's just a quarter to six. Good morning.

Have just got up and will finish this curious production while waiting for breakfast. I see none of the others yet, so my energy is not impaired, you see. How did you get back from Dunleary? Quite well I hope, and I hope also that you were not and are not too lonely. I always think when I've left you how much nicer I ought to have been to you. Do you think that about me when I am gone? Was sorry this morning that I hadn't that dressing gown. Fixed up in very nice quarters here — bedroom, bathroom and sitting room all in a little nook by themselves. You'd love them.

Goodbye for the day dear dear Kit and God Bless you.

Mícheál.

Letter 96

Kitty, to Mícheál, Saturday, no date, no indication of when received.

Sweetheart,

Your letter to-day was a lovely surprise, also the little boy in *The Sketch*.[1] I wish you were here. But next week I hope to see you, perhaps Tuesday or Wednesday. This is a lovely day, and I'm in good form. Rushing for post, so excuse this.

Bye bye, my own love. Don't work too hard, and write on Monday anyway.

This time this day week I was feeling so excited. You were not far away!

Yours with love,
Kit.

1. *The Sketch*, a London pictorial magazine.

Letter 97

Mícheál, London, to Kitty, 21 January 1922.

Kitty darling,

I have just returned at 3.45 from a four hours interview with Sir James Craig.[1] You'll probably see our agreement published in the morning's paper, but I'm not sure if it will be in time. At any rate I am writing this note as it seems a long time since I wrote in the morning and that's that and slán leat and everything.

Fondest love,
Mícheál.

1. James Craig, first Viscount Craigavon (1871-1940). He organised the Ulster Volunteers for armed resistance to home rule, was the first Prime Minister of Northern Ireland, and author of the saying that Stormont was 'a Protestant parliament for a Protestant people'.

Letter 98

Mícheál, Dublin, to Kitty, 23 January 1922.

K. dearest,

That ap.[1] is made for the Dolphin[2] at 2 o'clock today. Where may I meet you at that time — or will you come to the Dolphin and I'll wait for you at the door, or will you say any better place where I can pick you up and bring you there?

Love,
M.

1. Appointment.
2. A well-known Dublin hotel and restaurant near the City Hall and Dublin Castle.

Letter 99

Mícheál, Dublin, to Kitty, 27 January 1922.

Kitty dearest,

Just one word only. I am really and truly having an awful time and am rapidly becoming quite desperate. Oh Lord, it's honestly frightful.

How are you? I'm looking forward to your letter in the morning. Did you get home safely? And were you met all right? Have you been lonely since? At any rate I have and I was very cross with myself last night and had the idea all the time that you got into a depressed mood over something I said to you. Please forgive me if that is so. Slán leat my Kit.

> Fondest love,
> Mícheál.

Letter 100

Kitty, to Mícheál, in the train at Mullingar, received Friday evening, 27 January 1922.

My very dear M,

Am trying my new pen. It's a glamorous little outfit, and I *am* pleased with it. How I wish with all my heart that you were just here on the train where no one could be looking for you or take you away from me.

I feel so very very sad and lonely too. It is a mistake to love any one too much. But it cannot be undone, and at any rate I have the little ring which means you. But if it was only you, and not the ring! But isn't life full of ifs? I would be oh! so happy going away from you now, if only I knew or thought you were not overworking yourself, and having rest. It is a hard problem to solve. Perhaps after all one day I may have you to myself (and, I hope, in this world!!!). Did you ever think that it was unfair to me not to mind yourself better? Ducky, don't be vexed with me, but I have a great selfish love for you, no, not really *very* selfish, but a longing, such a longing, to be yours entirely and you mine. When will it be? I won't be content *then* with odd hours. You will just have to stay and mind your own me. And how

I hope this note (bad and all as it looks) will be a surprise
to you and that you get it to-morrow.

> Bye Bye till Sunday,
> Your pet and everything,
> Kit.

I'm feeling better since I wrote this, but lonely, lonely.
Curse shaky hand. My heart is sad till we meet again, and
then it will be sad if you look and feel tired. But I don't
blame you, ducky. Please do forgive me if I worry you.

Letter 101

Kitty, to Mícheál, Friday, received 28 January 1922.

My own dear sweetheart,
    Hope you got my letter this morning, posted in Mullingar
last night. I was hoping it would be a little surprise for you,
and although I was feeling tired in the train I was anxious to
write to you. Got home safely. Mops was ready to greet me
and had heard about ring from G.[1] She is mad about it,
thinks it's absolutely *IT*, and so do all my friends. She went
off to Enniskillen to-day. So one is all alone. But picture
my anxiety to see you again, especially as I wasn't half nice
enough to you when leaving. You will excuse my little fit,
but you know that my heart is all right, and that I want
really to make you happy even tho' sometimes I am so queer,
and don't show you my real feelings; but you guess, and that
is the salvation.
    How are you? Poor old you who really do not like my
sympathy; but if it would have been of any use to you, you
have a queer old lot of it from me. All I wish is that I could
really make you happy. Perhaps, after all, sometime I do
anyway. I often try to get your mind off work and worry
and try to please you. Now don't I, even tho' for the first
time for a long time I am displeased with myself and sorry
I don't act differently when in town, and allow you more
rest and sleep? But you'll see what a good girl I'll be in
future, and not what I like or what you like, but what is
right for us. Some revolution! Perhaps you'll dread coming

to Granard now that you've read this, but I want to put my own little mind to rest, and it never will be until I feel that I do right. Just wait and see if I don't be your very own love, and you will be pleased with me and glad you came, as the house will be quiet if you come Saturday night, and I'll meet you *myself*.

I enclose Seán's[2] letter to me. I can't reply yet until you decide. Apart from a selfish reason, I do think it would be far the wisest thing not to motor down on Sunday, and then have to go off to a party same evening, but do come on Saturday night. Lord knows the least you may have is Saturday night and Sunday. So please wire to-morrow so that I can wire Seán or the Cooneys[3] and perhaps Larry and I could motor you over, and Seán mightn't come here.

Now, dear, don't forget to wire and do try to come. I'll have a fire in bedroom, and no one to talk to. Have a lot of news for you, and Seán will be charmed to have you, and so pleased that you came.

Bye bye. Hope to have a letter in the morning. Good bye and love and kisses from yours as ever,

Kit.

Please keep Seán's letter for me.

1. Gearóid O'Sullivan.
2. Seán MacEoin.
3. The family of Alice Cooney, Seán MacEoin's bride to be.

Letter 102

Mícheál, Dublin, to Kitty, 29 January 1922.

My own dearest Kitty,
I was very very sorry that I had to wire you as I did yesterday but unfortunately there was no way out for me. Am writing this at the office and I have to attend an important conference at 2, so you have to suffer. Next week end will be much the same, but I must go down one evening during the week — that is if the trains are running — and come back the next morning. It will be seeing you in any case and that's something.

You'll be seeing from the papers that the Sinn Féin clubs are going strongly Republican — and the places: such places! Tralee after the Auxies[1] had gone, Galway the same. God help us from them. They're beauties.

Your letter of Friday was very delightful and I was awfully glad to get it. In a way I was more pleased to think of you writing on that train. It reminded me of the little notes I wrote in similar circumstances myself. Very pleased also that that little representative of mine meets with approval.

I had spent the last hour or so writing an article for an American newspaper and now I'm going to the 2 o'clock affair. Very hard but I'm in good form. Have had a good sleep or two since.

Don't be worrying about town. All my fault. Mary[2] is in love with you. Is that any use to you? I didn't see her afterwards. God bless you.

My fondest love always,
Mícheál.

Am wondering what you're doing this minute. Are you going to McK Killashee[3] tonight?

Bye bye,
M.

1. Members of the notorious Auxiliary Division of the Royal Irish Constabulary, formed in July 1920.
2. His sister, Mary Collins-Powell.
3. McKeon's (anglicised form of MacEoin) of Killashee.

Letter 103

Kitty, to Mícheál, 28 January 1922, telegram.

Going to Killashee to-morrow. K.

Letter 104

Kitty, to Mícheál, Monday, received Tuesday 31 January 1922.

My very dear M,

This letter will be short, but I'll write a long one to-morrow.

I'm feeling very sleepy after dance. Larry and I went to
Killashee. It was a very wet night, and I didn't feel a bit
like going. However, I did it for you. Surely it was a labour
of love if you only knew. Seán and all the crowd were there.
They were nice people and tried to make it pleasing for us.
His girl is nice. They were so disappointed you were not there
— and I wasn't let forget you! So, when I was feeling bored,
I had that to ~~distract me~~[1] help me to enjoy it. That word
'distract' I thought I'd better alter, in case you might take
the *wrong* meaning of the word!

Delighted with your letter to-day. It certainly helped to
cheer me up.

I am looking forward to seeing you, if only for an evening.
Be prepared to have to listen to a long talk from me. I was
going to write it, but now that you are coming I'll wait. Much
better indeed. Hope you keep in good form.

> Bye bye, dear,
> Fondest love,
> from Kit.

The tea party was an all-night dance. Had you been, you
would have been made dance, I believe.

1. The words 'distract me' are crossed out exactly like this in Kitty's
   original letter.

Letter 105
Mícheál, Dublin, to Kitty, 31 January 1922.

Kitty dearest,

I am writing this while all my Government[1] are waiting
for me. Your letter has been giving me concern. What are you
going to *talk* to me about?

Was at the Requim Mass for the Holy Father today.[2] Said
a full rosary for you alone.

Goodbye dear. Hope to see you Thursday night.

> Fondest love,
> Mícheál.

1. Apart from Collins, the Provisional Government originally consisted
   of W. T. Cosgrave, E. J. Duggan, Kevin O'Higgins, Eoin MacNéill,
   Fionan Lynch, P. J. Hogan and Joseph McGrath.
2. Pope Benedict XV.

Letter 106

Kitty, to Mícheál, Tuesday, received 1 February 1922.

My very dear M,

Sorry to know from your letter today that you are so worried and overworked. It is really very sad, especially from my point of view. But everyone is talking about you, how marvellous you are, and how wonderfully well you are running things. There was quite a sensation here when yourself and Craig met. People were stunned, and charmed, and the place is full of Belfast travellers, my old friends from the Hotel. They were mostly Northerners we had coming.

I suppose George went to Enniskillen. I haven't heard from Mops yet.

Your letter yesterday was very nice — it's a shame to be working on a Sunday. Killashee was all right, but I don't enjoy those functions.

Yes, the Sinn Féin clubs are amusing.

What night will you come? I am most anxious to see you. Would you bring a parcel which is in the Gresham for me from Miss Brennan.[1] She hadn't my navy coat ready when I was leaving, so I said that to send it to the Gresham would do; if you had come on Sunday, you could have taken it along here. So please take it from there, when you have time, and bring it to me.

Nothing new here. I am just as usual. Glad Mary liked me. She is a fine type. Has Harry got back yet? Wire what night you are coming. Of course if you can't get away I'll understand and forgive you. I must only be resigned to my lot. Bye bye.

Fondest love from,
Kit.

1. A dressmaker who had a shop in Grafton St and later in Dawson St.

Letter 107

Mícheál, Dublin, to Kitty, 1 February 1922.

My own dear Kitty,

Your letter received this morning all right. The usual grateful thanks.

Am definitely going down tomorrow evening by the 7.30 train and returning on Friday morning. Am running now to catch Hynes[1] and Paddy Cusack for half an hour. Feeling better and I hope I shall be in good form for you tomorrow. You also.

God be with you.

Fondest love,
Mícheál.

1. Not identified.

Letter 108

Kitty, to Mícheál, Wednesday, received Thursday 2 February 1922.

My very dear M.,

Delighted to hear from your letter to-day that you may be down on to-morrow night. You mustn't worry about me. This has been a glorious day here and I was out for a long walk.

To-morrow will be an exciting day for Dublin when Craig arrives. I wish you good luck with your Conference.

I have absolutely no news, so you will have to excuse short letter. Larry is away at a coursing match up in Trim with Peggie, so I am quite alone to-day. One misses the large family we did have at a time like this.

It was very good of you to say a whole Rosary for me.

Now I'll say good-bye till to-morrow night, D.V.

Fondest love,
Kit.

Wire what train. If it should be Edgeworthstown you thought of, Streete is a much better road to meet you, and not a mile in the difference.

K.

Letter 109

Sinéad de Valéra, Greystones, Co. Wicklow, to Mícheál, 3 February 1922, translation.

Dear Mícheál,

I got your letter this morning telling me that £50 had

been paid into my bank account. But we should not get money now, since Éamon is no longer president since last month.

I am sending you a cheque for £50.

I am very grateful to you, and I shall never forget all you always did for me.

With every blessing and kind regards,
> I remain,
> Your friend always,
> Sinéad de Valéra.

Collins retained the loyalty of the majority of the GHQ of the IRA, of his intelligence corps, and the Squad, as well as men like Seán MacEoin, but a majority perhaps of the IRA throughout the country went on the other side, among them units that had done little or nothing in the war with the British. The situation was broadly the same within Sinn Féin as the clubs prepared for an ard-fheis which was to discuss the Treaty. In the meantime, however, the British evacuation continued, barracks were handed over to IRA officers irrespective of their views on the Treaty and some of these men disregarding GHQ, commandeered foodstuffs and transport, seized monies from post offices and suppressed newspapers whose opinions did not accord with their own. To make things worse, a few British soldiers, waiting to be evacuated, were shot, and Collins had to face criticism on this score when he went to London to discuss the transfer of government services, the Ulster issue, or the 'thoroughly democratic' Constitution of the Irish Free State with which he hoped to win over a sizeable number of 'republican' dissidents. The Northern problem had not become any easier as a consequence of the further talks with Craig.

Letter 110

Mícheál, Dublin, to Kitty, 3 February 1922.

My dearest Kit,

Got back safely and strange to say I am not feeling in the

least tired. Evidently 3 hours in Granard (sleep) is as good
as about 6 anywhere here. I have been immersed in things
ever since the moment I left you. The statement which is
appearing in the press this evening and tomorrow morning
I wrote in the train, and that's an indication of how I've
been going on. Am writing this at 4 p.m. and am wondering
what you're doing just now — have you got up? Perhaps
you're writing to me, but perhaps you've already done that
or perhaps you'll not write at all today.

Have been held up, badgered, all day since my return and
am off to a meeting now.

May God bless you,

Fondest love,
Mícheál.

Caught the train by two minutes. They saw us coming and
they waited. Usual luck for me, you'll say. *Usual luck for
you also*. Love again,

M.

Letter 111

Mícheál, Dublin, to Kitty, 4 February 1922.

My own dear Kitty,

Your very very small, very very scraggy note came safely
this morning, and it was indeed very welcome. Am looking
forward to that long letter on Monday but, alas, I won't
have it until Tuesday, I fear very very much.

All of a sudden I am called away to London. The Craig
business is serious, and if we don't find some way of
dealing with it, all the bravos will get a great chance of
distinguishing themselves once more.

I wish you were coming to London with me tonight.
I have been thinking about that trip for you and haven't
worked out anything really satisfactory. If I knew some
people going to the south of France would you go with them,
or would you go to Rome? Anyway I'll think more about it,
and do you also please [*sic*]. Must go to lunch and must do
millions of things by 7 o'clock.

With all my love, Kit dear,
Mícheál.

Are you in better form again? Don't be getting into those
queer fits.

> Love again,
> M.

Letter 112

*Mícheál, Jermyn Court Hotel, Piccadilly Circus, London, to
Kitty, Sunday morning, 5 February 1922.*

My own Kit,

We have just arrived here and I have sat down to write a
line before going to bed. Am in the same room as last time
I was here, and have a few lovely fires. It's awfully pleasant
as far as comfort goes, but I'm thinking of another fire — not
the stolen one but the fire we had all for ourselves last time
I was with you. Had a very good crossing and am feeling
quite refreshed. Slept practically the whole way on the train —
more sleep than I've had for many a night. In fact I am not
feeling a bit like going to bed now — but 'all the same' (as
we say in Cork) I'm off. Just thinking, it will be funny if you
get this before the letter I wrote in Dublin.

May God be with you.

> Fondest love,
> Mícheál.

Letter 113

*Mícheal, Jermyn Court Hotel, London, to Kitty, slightly later
that Sunday morning, 5 February 1922.*

Kitty dearest,

I'm completing now so that I may post to you before I
start the work of the day. Am waiting for breakfast, then
Mass, then conferences for the whole day. I hope to get
finished tomorrow and so to return tomorrow night. Things
do not appear to be very promising but perhaps it's a
question of 'being the darkest hour before the dawn'. At any
rate today will tell a great deal, and I suppose we shall have
something for the newspapers for the morning. I find I am

rambling on in a descriptive kind of way, and as I must not depart from my well-known failing of being most close-mouthed, I'll have to go off the bye path that may 'lead me astray'.

Goodbye for the day. I may write you again: I feel like writing a lot.

With fondest love,
Mícheál.

Letter 114

Kitty, to Mícheál, Monday, received 7 February 1922.

My very dear Mícheál,

Apologies for that little scraggy note. I was badly had as regards time on Friday — got up at 11 o'c, the day seemed to fly, went up to Cusacks by Paul's request to go for a walk and, while there, discovered it was five o'c, and so I scribbled that awful looking scrap. Had intended writing you a letter. Then on Saturday I was very busy. No post on Sundays. Please forgive me.

Was delighted to see you on Thursday, and it was great having that little chat. Only I must *never* go into your office. Written in large letters across my mind. Never, Never.

Sorry for you having that long run up to London. I hope you have good luck. Mops isn't back yet. She couldn't be allowed leave until next Wednesday. Something like my experience last time I was in town. Her salutation when I arrived in here, 'Oh, I thought Mick wouldn't allow you home for several days more.' Still I am only joking — but she wasn't.

Can't plan anything definite about my trip, sweetheart, until she, Mopsy, returns. Then I'll think seriously about it. Thank God I am feeling ever so much better since I saw you. See, what *you* can do, after all.

Rushing now, so bye bye. Shall write later, to-night perhaps.

Yours with love,
Kit.

Letter 115

Mícheál, Dublin, to Kitty, 7 February 1922.

My own dearest Kit,

I am just trying to write a line so that I may get the mail
train. Will have to send it to Broadstone specially. Got back
this morning and found your letter at the Gresham after I
woke up. Very very worn out today, but even so in pretty
good form. It's no use grumbling, Kit dear. It was certainly
very wrong of you not to have written that letter but I
suppose I must no longer find *any fault* with you now since
it seems somewhat like blaming myself. What do you think
of that? Am rushing to catch that train. Wish I were catching
it myself.

May God bless you always,

Fondest love,
Mícheál.

How is my little representative?[1]

1.The engagement ring perhaps.

Letter 116

Kitty, to Mícheál, 7 February 1922, received 8 February.

My very dear Mícheál,

Your London letters arrived safely to-day. I was very
pleased with them and delighted that you were in such good
form and slept a bit. I had almost pitied you having to go to
London for the week and the long cold journey, but your
letter sounded good, and I imagined the fires all right!

Had a very nice letter from Hannie which I'll answer
shortly.

Am sure you were disappointed when you got back and
found only one letter from me. I had really the good
intention to send you a long letter. Don't know what can
have happened. When you had gone Friday morning I wrote
you an unsent letter in imagination; am sure I must have
been an hour writing it. Such devotion and love. I do believe
you would have felt pleased and charmed and very happy. It

was my best attempt yet, but, sorry to say, the attempt to
write it was very bad.

I am anxious to see you again. I felt so happy and glad
the last morning you were here. When I am with you — not
near you! — I am always more or less content, but when we
are apart, a letter is the only thing in my day, or in life
after you. That's a bad stage, but I must blame myself.

Dearest pet, I shall be so delighted and excited if you do
come this week. I hate to build up hopes of your coming
in case they might collapse, so I try to keep calm, and look
forward to the day. Mops may come to-morrow, but once
Monday is over I don't mind, only I am lonely for her at
times. I wrote and told her to stay until Monday morning
and she took me at my word and stayed two days more.

Do try and come soon. All my bestest love, and a hug and
a kiss.

Yours,
Katti.

Will promise this time not to waste so much time, so that
we can go to bed early. It is really absurd my behaviour
and really all my fault in that way. Bye bye. Do you like
my new name? I'll tell you when you come what I read.
Katti.

Letter 117

Kitty, to Mícheál, Wednesday, received 9 February 1922.

My own dear sweetheart,

I felt very excited to-day when opening your letter. I
thought it might be to say that you were coming this
evening. Of course I became resigned as soon as possible.
I knew if you could you would come. You see, you said you
'might' on Wednesday or Thursday. But you know, ducky,
I am never unreasonable, and realise how overworked you
are. Indeed I was sympathising with you — in my own mind
— on your trip to London (although I didn't tell you)
because I thought you would be just dead when you would
get back, and all the excitement over. I dare not ask if you

had a good time, as you were not a whole day there. You are amazing how you can get around so quickly.

Your article on Monday's paper read very well, I thought.

No sign of Mopsy yet. I was too liberal. I'll go to meet you to-morrow night if by any chance you come. I do really hope that you have had some good sleeps since, and are feeling very fit. I'll promise not to lecture you any more, so you will just have to relie [*sic*] — can't spell — on yourself. Last night you were here I was always finding fault.

Your letter to-day was very nice. In fact, I liked all your letters lately. It was time that you should say a few little things. I'd love to write you pages and pages of things, but I just won't be too silly. Now, you will be furious. You'd love it. You would, wouldn't you? But don't I say the nice things — about 3 a.m. — enough to do you for days? I wish — am always wishing — that you were here now. I always want you near. Isn't that *something* to say?

And now good bye. With lots of kisses until perhaps to-morrow.

Your own little pet,
Kit.

Letter 118

Father Malachy, O.F.M., The Friary, Fox St, Liverpool to his cousin, Kitty, 9 February 1922, and enclosure.

My dear Kitty,

I must send you enclosed. But don't get too conceited over it. It is a cutting from the *Liverpool Express*, a deeply Orange and anti-Catholic paper.

Don't forget to answer my other letter.

Love to all,
Malachy, O.F.M.

The cutting, headed 'Where are the Beauties?', was a letter signed 'Ex-Service man', with an address in Wallasey. It read:

Sir, During the recent festivities it has been difficult to compare the many fairy-like scenes but, apart from the Royal Wedding and coming as it were in its train, one of the

115

prettiest pictures in the *Express* has been that of Miss Kitty Kiernan, the intended bride of the Financial Minister of the Irish Free State.

Not for a long time has the public been so highly favoured as by the good fortune of inspecting the picture of this lady, whose presence would grace the life of any man however highly placed, and whose inborn native beauty is portrayed in every outline of her life.

It was in Westmeath the writer[1] had the privilege of seeing her, in the days of the late war, and in a country of beautiful women the reputation is well retained by the choice of one whose sagacity has been so wisely proven in his efforts for the advancement of his native land.

The query naturally arises — To what country must we look for the most conspicuous ideals of Nature's beauties but amongst the daughters of our Sister Isle?

1. In Letter 143 Kitty identified the writer.

Letter 119

Kitty, to Mícheál, Wednesday night, received 10 February 1922.

My own lovie,

It is just 7 o'c and I've said good bye to the little shop for the day. One of the girls has a cold and was in bed to-day, so with Maud away I had to take the girl's place. Have just come in here and am writing to you before I have my tea. If by any chance you should come to-morrow this letter won't go, but if you don't, you will get it. How I wish you were here, ducky. I think I'd be nice to you, at least I'd do my best. You say I am very nice 'sometimes', but sure I don't ever get a chance of being nice to you.

I pity myself sometimes that I am so queer. I long to be all that I might be to you, but for these little fits. I will try so hard to overcome them because I know I'd be much happier if only I could be my real self with you. (This seems to be the beginning of a little book entitled 'The Secrets of the Heart'! However, I am in the mood for talking to you.)

116

Of course, I am much too sensitive, and too highly susceptible to anything you might or might *not* say, or to any of your actions. Lots of it may be imagination on my part, and it is I who suffer most perhaps, although I know it is hard on you too. While it lasts I get miserable. For instance, in Dublin at times you made me feel almost uncomfortable. I didn't know where I stood with you. I found myself wondering. You were, I know, overworked and tired. If only I could have left you alone, to yourself, until you recovered, but time seemed so precious from my point of view, and I hated not being absolutely with you, while with you. I was entirely at your mercy, lived for the time when we would meet again. All the days seemed empty until I had you. Then I was disappointed. Had I not set myself out to devote *all* my time to you, it would have saved the position and made it more comfortable for both of us really. But there's where I have to learn a lot. There is where I am young and inexperienced. I should have made a programme for myself, and not be entirely depending on you. But then the point comes in. To love you *at all* is a nuisance to you. I told you so before — no half-measures with me. (I do not tell you how I feel often, and try to overcome my feelings for you, ducky, with the obvious result.) But would it not be better in the long run if I could succeed now. There's the position.

On the *other* hand, I almost shudder at the thought of the strength of my love, what I do believe I am capable of feeling and that, without you, life held nothing for me. Nobody mattered to me, not even myself, if you were not with me. In other words it would mean just living for you. Then how to live *best* for you. To do justice to myself as well as to you is also a puzzle. Because I'll feel that if I do it for myself, it's for you. Every little thing would be for you as well as for me. I'd naturally like to feel happy, because I do believe that mood would affect you and make you happy. I think perhaps my unhappiness is purely from being run down etc., and that, please the Lord, can be altered when I get right away from the present surroundings, the horror of everything staring one in the face, and no way out of it.

And now I'll finish. I long for the time when I can be (as I used always to be) gay and light-hearted, and then I'll make big worries seem small, and small things nothing at all, and you will be my little world. I mean my world would be you, first. This is no foolish talk or imagination. And if only the day comes soon when I can thoroughly understand you, and even when, like in Dublin, I won't be so greedy, wanting you, wanting you, always and ever wanting you. And isn't it something nice for you to dream about, no matter how complicated it might at the time become? But not so pleasant at the time for

Your Kit.

Letter 120

Kitty, to Mícheál, Thursday, no indication of when received, probably on 11 February 1922.

My dear,

Wrote you enclosed last night. If you have *not* already read it, wait until to-night to do so. Have just read it over, and don't you think I had punch. It reads so silly to-day, to me at least.

See what you are getting by not coming to-night, a regular little book, but don't think that, if you don't come to-morrow night, you will get the same sort of book. Oh no.

Maud comes to-morrow. She was to come to-day, but I've just had a wire. By writing to you last evening, I don't have to write to-day. Some advantage gained!

Goodbye till Friday.

Yours ever,
Kit.

Excuse bad writing in other letter, but it was all written on my knee at fire.

Letter 121

Mícheál, Dublin, to Kitty, 10 February 1922.

My dearest Kit,

You'll be surprised to hear it but I was not displeased

with your letter written on Wednesday night. It was thoughtful, and made me think that I had not been explaining things sufficiently, and that that was the real reason you did not understand me.

Am going down tomorrow on the 1.30 and will go to Ballywillan.[1] Will you meet me please?

By the way here's an item of interest — I have drawn a cheque for £60 today. Do you know what it's for?[2] By another way you *must* be in good form — please dear dear Kit. When I meet you — and this much I'll ask also — you'll have to give me a couple of hours in the morning for work. Otherwise you'll have all my time. (I just see I can only go to Edgeworthstown[3] or Streete.[4] Will look out at both places.)

Several people clamouring for me. Do forgive this scraggy note. You don't know how anxious I am to see you. I have a kind of feeling that I must go away with you — strain telling on me also. May God be with you.

Fondest love,
Mícheál.

1. A station on the Midland Great Western Railway.
2. He was, we think, buying her a gold watch — see Letter No. 170.
3. and 4. Other stations on the MGWR.

Letter 122

Kitty, to Mícheál, Monday, received 14 February 1922.

Ducky,

Just a line. Will write you later. I never felt so happy as I do to-day, T.G. So I hope you are likewise. Everything seems good and cheery and I feel oh! so happy.

Bye bye,
My love to you,
Your own
Kit.

Whenever he could manage it at all, Mícheál strove to spend a week-end with Kitty in Granard. He was there during the second week-end in February and Kitty thrilled with happiness. He had introduced her to Omar Khayyam and quotes from the Fitzgerald translation of the *Rubaiyat* as he prepares in London for a hard day with Churchill. A letter from a relative of hers, Agnes O'Farrelly, lecturer in Celtic Studies at University College, Dublin, points to the dangers that face the country. In recent days there has been more trouble in the border area. Mícheál sees de Valera in a move to adjourn the Sinn Féin ard-fheis. Towards the end of February he has to lie up for a day with a heavy cold in the house of Miss McCarthy at 44 Mountjoy Street where he had been accustomed to stay, on and off, for many years. Kitty goes to see him there and comes away more anxious than ever that they should marry as soon as possible and have a place of their own where she could care for him herself. They had their eyes on a house in Greystones. She now has an engagement ring, and mentions some other 'things' Mícheál has given her, including a pen and pencil 'outfit'.

Letter 123

Mícheál, London, to Kitty, Wednesday, 15 February 1922.

My dearest Kitty,

All night travelling I was thinking and dreaming of you. It's all very pleasant and I am looking forward to our next meeting. Am going back tonight, I hope. That is my intention at any rate, and it will go very hard with me if I don't stick to it. I am just scribbling this before going to a conference with Mr Churchill and some of the others. Am expecting a pretty hard day but, like all other hard days, it will, I'm sure, come to an end all right.

How are you? I suppose you wouldn't have thought yesterday of writing to the Jermyn Court Hotel. It would be very pleasant to get a letter now but that, I fear, is not possible. Must finish up so as to get away. Hope you have kept in great form. Get happier and happier. Between us everything is just lovely now —

'. . . clear today of past regrets and future fears' —

Have you been reading Omar?[1] You've hardly got it by
this time. The other little book contains a few good things
also. They're on the sad side, but not melancholy.

Goodbye for today, dear dear Kit, and may we see each
other tomorrow.

My every wish and thought,
Mícheál.

1. Edward Fitzgerald's translation of *The Rubaiyat* of Omar Khayyam.

Letter 124

Kitty, to Mícheál, Tuesday, received 16 February 1922.

My very dear Mícheál,

I was sorry that I wasn't able to write to you at length
yesterday. When I was about to do so, of all people Miss
Dopping[1] called, and was very disappointed as we didn't
visit her lake. Better luck next time.

I was delighted with your letter to-day but sorry to know
you will have another visit to London. Poor you, you know
I am more than sorry. I hate to lecture you. If only Paul
wasn't there, nature would have seen to your sleep, and
before you realised it you would have been fast. However,
you seem to know that.

I am anxious to see you again. I love to have a little chat
with you. Maybe I will go up one evening, and then I'll be
satisfied with 1½ hours − perhaps − the first ½ to get used
to you.

I want to talk to you again. One of the things, about
drinking with H.B.[2] If he is *not* to be trusted in other things,
I wouldn't take much of that particular thing with him.
Enough said!

I wrote Chrys and said we would go up[3] week-end after
next, perhaps; so I hope you can work it in. It will be at the
end of the week. I may go up to town for one evening.

I am, I think, going to Roscommon for a dance to-morrow
night. Dr Delaney[4] called to-day and has coaxed me to go
with Mrs D and himself from Longford to-morrow evening,
motoring. It is going to be a grand affair, I hear. Don't

worry about me, now. I get better and better every time I see you, dearest sweetheart, and I feel ever so happy and pleased with you, and with me — self! Better still, and later on, I will go away. In due time, I hope, but can't decide yet.

Now bye bye, my own love, and be sure that I am yours no matter what comes. You are worth all — and more — that I could do for you.

Yours,
Kit.

In haste for post, writing this in shop; it's awful hard to do so! (Girl in bed with cold.) Larry is in Dublin and has my writing case for an attaché case. So, if you see it going around town, don't be surprised. I'll not go to town until Friday, and then this time I may visit dentist. Kisses and love.

K.

1. **Diana Dopping who resided at Derrycasson House near Lough Gowna. The Doppings were an old ascendancy family now apparently extinct.**
2. **Harry Boland.**
3. **To Bangor, Co. Down.**
4. **Dr Delaney, a G.P. in Church St, Longford.**

Letter 125

Mícheál, Dublin, to Kitty, possibly 16 February 1922.

My own dearest Kitty,

You see I am writing today as I intended to, before our conversation on the phone. The two days don't commence to run until I *don't* get a letter from you in the morning. I suppose you're in bed now — in that case I may not ring up although I had intended doing so — in fact I have asked them to try to get Dr Delaney. Isn't it a pity there isn't a phone in Granard, but you often go to places where there is a phone — don't you? Whenever you go to one of those places, will you please try to get on to me now that you know the number. It's 5345, extension 4.[1]

That was rather severe, what you said about H.[2] this

morning but I'm not so sure that your keen womanly 'horse sense' is not right. I have noticed a very uncommon instinct in you in that regard. It's better than my own often. It really is. Please do let me see you soon. Could you really not come tomorrow and stay for the week end. Not at the Gresham, and *not alone*.

All my love,
M.

1. This was his telephone number and extension at the City Hall.
2. Harry Boland.

Letter 126

Kitty, to Mícheál, Wednesday, possibly received on 16 February 1922.

My own sweetheart,

When I was just thinking of writing to you yesterday, who should land in but Dr and Mrs D? So your 'phone message had a bad result! They came to tell me what you said. Hard luck but I didn't get a chance of telling you what I thought of you. Of course, I didn't mind you not writing. A little disappointment like that is of no consequence — glad you think so.

Ducky, how are you this ages and ages? I feel I have been neglecting you by not going to see you long ago. You must be fading away from being so long without seeing me. Seriously, how are you? You never say. Tired and fed up I should imagine. Yes, I too wish that I was near you this week particularly, to give you a little hug, kiss etc. No lecture, of course. No!

I feel so sorry for you with those meetings and everything. But you know I do, and when I can't be with you to tell you so, you know I'm thinking of you and helping you in my mind. Very unsatisfactory this, and the longing to see you always there or nearly always. I left a space, meaning to fill in the word when I'd find in the dictionary how to spell it, in my last letter, and when I came back to it I couldn't remember what the word was. It was just posting time, so I was very badly had. The word then, when it was late was running through my head. It is 'contradictory', so you can fill it in in my letter. I know all the spare time you have! So it will help you to pass the time!!

When will I see you? I have the queerest feeling — if only you could walk into the room *now*. So long as I wouldn't have to wait in patience until you came. I simply couldn't wait, and, to look forward, the days would seem so beastly long. Could you not come just down to-morrow night? But, dearest lovie, if you can't, you can't. I'll go to town next week certain. Have you still the house in view? Mops may come with me to town for one day or so, so that's why I wait.

Then to-night I go to a dance in Cavan, and Friday night, perhaps, in Mullingar, and I'll write Chrys that we can't go to Bangor this week-end, as I said we might go in my letter. But if you can come down here towards the end of the week or to-morrow I'll be _____? Could you guess?

Do try your best, and good bye my love, my own love. With heaps of love, hugs, and everything nice. Your own little pet,

Kit.

I was at Roscommon and danced all night and wore the Hoops. Some 'figure' I looked.

Letter 127

Kitty, to Mícheál, Friday, received 18 February 1922.

My dear Mícheál,

Please excuse pencil. Got back here [Granard] about 9 o'c last evening I went to bed about 2 o'c and slept till 4 o'c, so that's all the sleep I had.

I enjoyed the dance muchly as usual. Dr and Mrs Delaney were very decent to me and we had a great night. I am sure you were surprised when I 'phoned you. Would love to have talked longer but you were busy I knew; and I might have gone to town this week only for the dance. I only knew I was going, the evening before the dance.

The little books arrived the day I went, so I didn't have time to enjoy them yet. Thanks very much. I was just delighted to get them, and they do me as well as large ones. Also thanks for both your letters.

Suppose you will be annoyed that I didn't write, but really I don't know why I didn't. I was very lonely yesterday evening for you after I *heard* your voice and got a longing to see you, and then depressed that fate was so unkind, you 70 miles from me, and never able to see you when I most wanted you. But sure I should be accustomed to that by now, but it's very hard sometimes, you know. I love you as much as ever, so perhaps you can imagine then how much I miss you *always*.

Peggie is here now. She and Larry went to Longford dance same night as I went to Roscommon. She is away in Kells coursing with him to-day. I know no pair have such a time as she and Larry have.

Larry met Harry in town. Harry said he was coming, but Larry doesn't know the day, I think. However, I didn't ask Larry. I forgot. It was Peg told me.

I wish we could meet soon, but please the Lord, I'll go to town next week, but not to the Gresham. I'll not have a letter from you until Monday — that will be the *two* days, Saturday and Sunday. So I'll be very lonely. I'll keep all the news till I see you.

So bye bye. Writing this on my knee. So excuse, dearest, Good bye.

> Yours as ever,
> Kit.

Letter 128

Mícheál, Dublin, to Kitty, 17 February 1922.

Kitty dearest,

1. The two days start from tomorrow morning. They are Saturday and Monday.

2. The stamp on this was the first Free State stamp ever licked by a member of the Free State Provisional Government. That much for you — it was, of course, licked by me for you.

3. Tried to get you on the telephone at 8.30 last night, but failed. You had gone.

4. Goodbye for as many days (so far as letters go) as *you* decide.

> All my love,
> my dear dear Kit,
> Mícheál.

Letter 129

Agnes O'Farrelly, 26 Highfield Rd, Rathgar, Dublin, to Kitty, 20 February 1922.

Dear Kitty,

. . . How have you been since? You have been in Dublin and did not come to see me? I thought we had arranged you were to let me know and both of you were to come for a nice quiet couple of hours away from the noise and worry of things. We shall be delighted to see you both, and Maudie also if she is in town any time.

Things are beginning to look very serious. It will require a great deal of wisdom and understanding to keep the country — or a section of it — from heading straight for civil war.

Kind remembrance to Maudie (you are becoming a very small family now — only two left) and to your fiancé. . . .

Letter 130

Mícheál, Dublin, to Kitty, 20 February 1922, telegram.

Wonder would it be possible for you to come up evening train. Am lying up to-day but only fagged out and may have to go to London to-morrow night. Reply 44 Mountjoy Street.
> Mícheál.

Letter 131

Mícheál, Dublin, to Kitty, 21 February 1922.

My own dearest Kitty,

You will kill me (but not rightly) for not receiving a letter

this morning. I was with de V yesterday from 4 until 8.30.
It was because of that you didn't get the letter which I
wanted to write to you, and which was and is your right.
Now this won't make up for it, but I do hope that you'll
be in a good humour today, and that consequently you
won't be very disturbed at not hearing. At any rate I phoned
Longford with a kind of order to tell you I couldn't write.
I want to see you and that's that. I do want to see you —
Kitty Kiernan, I do badly. Just away from Sinn Féin árd-fheis
for an hour's interval. Isn't it nice to think of you in every
free moment — oh! and in moments that are not free too?
    God be with you, my dear, dear Kitty.

All my love,
Mícheál.

Letter 132

Mícheál, Dublin, to Kitty, 22 February 1922

My dear dearest Kitty,
    I'm writing this to you today first to let you know that
I'm feeling very disappointed at not hearing from you today.
It was not fair of you.

With all my love,
Your very own —
(if you want it) —
Mícheál.

Letter 133

*Mícheál, Irish Provisional Government, City Hall, Dublin, to
Kitty, 23 February 1922.*

My dear dearest Kitty,
    Very delighted with your letter this morning. I am kind of
sorry I wrote that note yesterday — probably it will have
hurt you. Am very anxious to see you — oh Lord how
anxious. More keen than you now. Goodbye for the moment,
and everything.

Your own,
Mícheál.

Letter 134

Kitty, to Mícheál, Monday, received 22 February 1922.

My very dear Mícheál,

Watched for the post very eagerly to-day. I don't know why. One moment I would think he will write, then, no, he won't, until the time *at last* came. So you see that by doing the good child, you are getting a letter from me! Otherwise, I'd probably be thinking I was too busy to-day, couldn't get a minute to write, etc. etc! But sure my own lovie of last Monday morning week — not about 2 o'c but just before — wouldn't disappoint me, and he knows that that's what she would do if she threatened not to write, give him a good surprise by writing. Of course her threats end in something too nice even to imagine.

I wrote on Saturday. I was just thinking that that was perhaps the anniversary of the first Saturday I ever wrote to you, and I do hope it was a great great surprise to you, as you don't often know of me on a Monday. I told you last time those days were years and I couldn't reconcile myself to write — it might be only acknowledging that they weren't your days and they were. Can't be content Saturday, Sunday and Monday morning until I have seen you. Some funny feeling came over me on Saturday evening last that it wasn't Saturday at all, and I didn't get over that until the letter was written. This is quite true. Of course I was delighted then, and hope you got it on Sunday morning.

It is ever so long since you were here. I am longing — such a longing — to see you, but feel I'll be selfish and go on wanting you all the time. It gets harder and harder every day. Am putting off going to town every day to see if I could get over the feeling, but I am afraid the longing is only increasing. Wish, wish, wish you felt the same.

What did you do yesterday, and last night? Had a most awful dream about you, and I awoke 'barging' you. But forgot *you* don't know the meaning of that word. Will *explain* it to you when we meet. Maybe this week, if I take a sudden fit, I'll go to town. Must surely see the dentist, and altogether am going to have a most uninteresting time.

I'll stay with Mrs Davis[1] and you can only — let me

break the news gently — visit me between the hours of
6 and 9 o'c at her flat. Have been trying to break the news
to myself first, but it's the devil!

Good bye. All the love and kisses that I cannot give you
when I see you I send now so that you may have them in
good time.

I'll cork the bottle, and say Bye Bye.

Yours lovingly,
Kitty Kiernan,
and one Big Hug.

1. This may have been Vi Davis's mother.

Letter 135

*Kitty, to Mícheál, Thursday, received Friday, 24 February
1922.*

Dearest,

Just a line before I go off to dreamland. M. & I went to
dance and enjoyed it. I stayed up most of the day but am off
now, feeling down and out.

By the way, *you* must have been also in dreamland
yesterday! — judging by the manuscript and appearance
generally of 'my letter' to-day. Now *don't* get annoyed —
could not make out one word of it! There was great joy in
Dublin yesterday I'm sure.[1] Tell Harry that I said he needn't
be afraid to come now, and that I am writing to him and that
we are expecting him here every day.

You must be glad of the agreement, as well as the rest of
Ireland.

Excuse short note, dear.

Fondest love, from
Sleepy Kitty.

1. A reference perhaps to the Collins-de Valera pact.

Letter 136

*Mícheál, Dublin, to Kitty, Sunday 26 February 1922 ('I
think')*[1]

My own dearest Kit,

You'll be glad to know that I slept fairly well from about

11 o'clock on, and am as a result feeling fairly well today. (My hand is a bit strange to writing already.) Am going into the sun for an hour, as it's very fine, and I feel it will do me much good. May write you another note when I return.

How did you get back? I do hope that I shall never again be in bad form when I see you. It's so frightfully unfair to you as I do feel I'm a changed being, and that's that. It's about 1. Car is waiting for me so I'd better get out and get back again as quickly as I can.

With all my love to you, Kit dear,
Your
Mícheál.

1. This appears, after the date, in Collins's hand in the original.

Letter 137

Mícheál, Dublin, to Kitty, 27 February 1922.

My own dearest Kitty,
As I said to you today that I might write again when I returned I am doing so to say that I have made my short journey — saw Nancy O'Brien[1] and Johnny. (Nancy isn't really well herself either in reality.) J. is in very good form. He slept well last night and is full of hope today. He is really to be admired in the cheerful way he takes things. *Family failing.* What *do* you think of that? All this is to say that the outing has done me great good and if you saw me now you'd see a changed man from this time yesterday — and I wish oh! how much I wish you were here with me.

I wonder what exactly you are doing at this precise moment? — it's just 4.30. Soon after the time you came back yesterday. Perhaps you have just written to me if you are not too tired today. And I hope, even if you've lectured me, that you do not think too badly of me for all my headstrong ways and my bad temper, and my impatience at being given good advice. But then I was in really bad form and if those traits of mine were worse than they are ordinarily, you'll forgive me — my dear Kit — *sure* you will? And you won't really misjudge me, will you? How long do you remain in town? If you have to go away before the week end

I'll make myself available, if humanly possible, to go wherever you are going — and that's that, and all my love to you again.

Your own,
Mícheál.

1. Nancy O'Brien, a cousin, was Johnny's second wife.

Letter 138

Mícheál, Dublin, to Kitty, 27 February 1922.

My dearest Kit,

Am at the office today and feeling ever so much better although I am kind of sorry that I wasn't able to stay in bed another day — it would have been good for me.

Your flowers looked lovely this morning when I woke up. They have kept wonderfully even in the hot room. That I regard as being a good sign.

There was no letter from you this morning — too busy, too something at any rate. But if you only knew how disappointed I was, you wouldn't really do those things. Am at this present moment rushing off to a meeting in the Mansion House but, as it may last longer than I expect, I am not chancing leaving writing you until afterwards.

Paul was in with me again yesterday. He had rather a nasty accident last night, I have just heard, but is getting on well. Helen has been sent for. Will let you know how he goes on. No good blaming him yet!

Must be gone. Hope you're writing today.

All my love,
Mícheál.

Letter 139

Kitty, to Mícheál, Monday night, received 28 February 1922.

My own dear Mícheál,

There is no post going out to-day, and I am so sorry that you can't have this in the morning. The train was too crowded to write a letter last evening. Larry, Paul etc. were on train also. We all got home safely, T.G.

Am thinking ever since how you are getting on. Of course, my coming home had the inevitable result. Why did I come, why didn't I stay with you? But really I did feel helpless while there. I could do absolutely nothing for you, and the idea in my mind all the time was that you would be better alone. There is not — nor should there be — any necessity to tell you how I felt about you. I was a bit of an invalid myself, and so didn't feel inclined to tell you all the nice things that I felt and were left unsaid. You will understand and forgive your own little me. *I* felt all the time that I'd love to be physically able to wrap you up in a big rug or something and carry you off to somewhere nice, far far away from 44 — yes, from 44, very far — to where there was wooded scenery, and large windows, the birds singing, and me in good humour, and where you could get a little breeze from the sea — or even the smell of the sea — and then a whole lot of other little things, the small things which also count.

I think I would be happy to-day if I knew that you had gone to even a nice nursing home, and that you slept all last night. I don't consider that you will really do Ireland or the people of Ireland any good by killing yourself working. You only do them an injustice. You are the one that, by living for Ireland, helps her. And then the injustice you will do me, sweetheart. We both clearly understand that any pain you may have is also mine, and any pain you might endure through not sleeping is just the same as if I were suffering. Your worries are my worries, your joys are my little joys, your happiness mine. When you are happy I am happy, no matter what I may say or pretend.

Unfortunately I amn't [*sic*] always my real self with you, but I do feel that, whenever I am my real self, you love it best of all. It is that which appeals most to you. I am confident of this; in other words I have confidence in myself. I keep keeping it reserved for you which unfortunately is a mistake sometimes — not to give the rosies all the time — but there is something strange in me which sometimes makes me find it hard to understand myself. It really is Reserve.

All my life I was a little like that with my nearest and dearest, tho' to those who don't really know me, I appear quite the opposite. It's a case of what I read being true. How little we know of those we know a lot, and what a lot we know of those we know a little.

Ever since I came back I have been thinking of your suggestion, and I went to the chapel to-night to pray for you and during that time thought that making the little sacrifices are no use if I couldn't make the big ones, and so it's June, D.V. Now I don't mean it's really a sacrifice in that sense, but just putting it off until I'd be ready also, etc., etc. Why not do the duty which lies nearest to me — to both of us — and be married in June? And so *Now* I have proposed to you! Are you satisfied? My weak inclination might be to put it off from month to month, but what I suggest is far the best for you, for me perhaps, and for both of us. I'll do my best to be good and strong by June D.V. and then you will at last have a responsibility; but I only want to be your little pet, your little child, your real pet, and, of course, your Duckie. That should come first, at least the way you say it. I want to be a million things to you.

I have heaps of little things to tell you when we are together, and I do believe it will be all I want if only I keep strong. That seems sometimes a little barrier. If it was got over, I feel I could do anything, and my longing would not be in vain. You know my longing, that I may fulfil all the part in life's little drama successfully for you and me. It's a big lot to expect. Nothing like looking for the big things anyway.

I must stop and say good night as I feel tired and sleepy. Will post this on first post tomorrow. You may yet get it sometime tomorrow. I send you a magazine I had in the train. If you are still in bed, read what amused me.

Will go to town on Wednesday, D.V., and please do your best to rest until then. Then a week somewhere — not sometime.

It's a great idea writing single pages, looks volumes this letter. Must write to Miss McC.[1] my thanks.

By bye, my lovie.

From your little sweetheart, lovingly,
Kit.

Travelled with my friend Mr Barry[2] again last night. He is
one of the nicest boys I have ever known. I have asked him
to visit *us* sometime.

Write me something nice to cheer me. Something about
your own dear self. You are all and only you. I am not
extra nice to you when you are in bad shape. Love, good
bye, my lovie, lovie.

1. Miss Myra T. McCarthy of Grianán na nGaedheal, the Munster Private
Hotel, 44 Mountjoy St.
2. Kitty's youthful friend, not Tom Barry of guerilla fame. See Letter 32.

Letter 140

Kitty, to Mícheál, Monday, received 28 February 1922.

My own dear M,

Excuse pencil. Writing in shop. Glad to get your note
to-day. I wrote you a big epistle last night late. I think
to-day maybe it was too long?

I am ever so pleased that you had sleep somehow. I had
confidence in Dr Ryan's[1] visit, not to speak of your nice
nurse and massage (can't spell) — which perhaps you didn't
have. You needn't apologise for your form. I only expected
it and knew that some fine day we'd have to pay the penalty
for all those nights we both had.

I must go to Athlone to-morrow and to town on Wednesday
or Thursday.

Love, yours,
Kit.

1. One of the doctors Mícheál had recommended.

Letter 141

Kitty, to Mícheál, Wednesday, received 2 March 1922.

Dearest,

We are going to town to-morrow and I'll phone you
sometime. Anyway we are sure to meet.

Hope you are feeling very well again. Now don't be a
fool and work too hard, if you can.

134

I got no letter to-day but suppose you thought I'd be up. We didn't go to Athlone either.

All my love until I see you. Will keep all news until to-morrow evening.

Most anxious to see you. We will have lots to talk about now.

Our house to start. I'm getting quite interested already. Are you?

Bye,
Love from
'Me'.
Your very own.

———————

Some of Kitty's letters from this period are written on notepaper that bears the monogram 'K'. In March, exactly two months after the betrothal announcement in the Dáil, a further public reference was made to the fact, and photographers descended on Kitty in Granard, and pictures of her in an evening gown were widely published: 'my old black evening dress', no doubt. In that month, as the result of the seizure by the anti-Treaty IRA of buildings in Limerick, GHQ called off a proposed army convention. One was held, nevertheless, confirming the split in the army. As it became necessary to ensure popular support, Collins increased the number of his public meetings. He spoke in Cork city in mid-March, and went from there to Charleville, Killarney, Tralee and Castlebar. He had to go to London, too, with his colleagues for another discussion with Craig on North/South relations. The general situation was lamentable, but Kitty's concern is mostly about Mícheál's health. It is becoming more apparent than ever that her own health is far from good.

Letter 142

Kitty, to Mícheál, Thursday, received 10 March 1922.

Dear very dear Mícheál,

Hope you got back all right. I got up at 11 o'c and then

135

spent an hour hunting for one of my stockings, going about one on and one off. You should see me. My glad rags got scattered about from room to room. Wish you could have stayed. This is a good day only it's very cold.

How do you do since and now? May I say I hope you *are* lonely. Not too lonely but just lonely. That does me. You will be so rushed and busy you won't have time to be too lonely.

Are you sorry you couldn't stay now? I had to laugh at myself this morning when I examined my conscience. What *could* I do if I had you here all day? But if I had you I'd DO, and I would never think of such a thing.

Bye bye. I send you my very bestest love. It is so long since I wrote to you now that it seems queer at first.

Shall write a long long one later.

Love. Good bye. Kisses and hugs,

Your own little pet,
Kit.

Letter 143

Kitty, to Mícheál, Friday, received 11 March 1922.

Dearest sweetheart,

Your letter to-day was very welcome. Am enclosing the Fr. Malachy one. Don't lose cutting, *please*. I want the only nice thing of me!

I think I know that officer who used to know me. Major Harris,[1] whom I met at private dances up here. Your cutting was very interesting.

I send you all my love (or nearly all) and everything. Excuse this and bye bye. Will write longer one later. Am going walking.

Yours,
Kit.

I liked your letter. You are a dote (sometimes). Hugs.

1. See Letter 118.

Letter 144

Kitty, to Mícheál, Saturday, received 13 March 1922.

My very dear Mícheál,

Have just been playing cat and dog with Lil.[1] Great sport we had! Outside the window her big sister was playing with another kiddie. 'Who are you?' one said, 'I am Miss Kitty, and you? ' The other said 'I am Mr Collins.' I had to laugh to myself. You would have laughed too.

Glad to get your letter to-day but sorry to know you were so busy. Poor old Ducky. I wish I could be of use to you, and I wish I was in your office now. Would I work? I mightn't. One never knows but I'd be there anyway and near you and I might be content.

Hope you have had a few good sleeps since and keep your promise to me? As for me, I feel just topping, and I'll do what you say, just for you, absolutely. Because when I feel A1 I am great and get full of confidence that you and I shall be the greatest of pals and everything. Really I *am* a different person when I get to that state. Have only been in that state a few times altogether since 'we met'. It was no imagination with me the doctor's visit. I am too sensible a person ever to suffer from imagination of that kind. I have a contempt for those who do. It was just the thing to do, only I'm sorry it was not ages ago I went.

When do we meet? It is years and years. This is a heavenly evening, and I wish — can you guess — what I wish so much?

Be good to thy self sometime — at least so that eventually there *will* be some of you left for me and not all gone on work and Ireland. The others thought you looked dreadfully tired that night in Cusacks. I cease to notice it as it only adds to my little worry.

Hope you do well in Cork, and that you gave them my regards etc.

With bestest love,
from 'Me'.

---

1. Lil, her big sister, and the other kiddie were neighbours' children in Granard.

Letter 145

Mícheál, Cork, to Kitty, 13 March 1922, telegram.

We had great days here. No chance of writing at all. Returning to Dublin to-night. How are you?

Mícheál.

Letter 146

Kitty, to Mícheál, Monday, received 14 March 1922.

My own lovie,

Delighted to get your wire to-day especially as I saw the papers since. We went to the lake yesterday and into the woods at Miss Diana Dopping's. Such a day. Lovely log fire when we returned, after we had gone through the woods (Paul and I). The others sat at the fire all the time. Not so daring!

I hope to be in town this week and to see you. Shall tell you all my little news then, and I wish that you would compose a little piece for me telling the press that I'll take an action against them if they continue to publish the rot they are writing. Did you see the *Irish Record*.[1] Nothing should go into any papers without my permission. Such lies and stories. It is quite time now to stop it.

Give my love to my sweetheart. *You* know 'who' that is. Also hugs and kisses. Excuse this scribble.

Always your own,
Kit.

Your speech read *great*, I thought.
P.S. How's poor old Ducky?

1. As far as we know there was no *Irish Record*. Kitty may have been thinking of some other 'Irish' paper.

Letter 147

Kitty, to Mícheál, received 15 March 1922.

My dear sweetheart,

Seán and his girl were here to-day and he said you had

great times in Cork. Ned Cooney[1] gave me full details.
Believe you had a large family into bed! Were they as good
and quiet as me?

Please excuse short note but I made a mistake in the
hour, and it's much nearer post time than I imagined.

The Barrack here was taken over to-day. It is a lovely
day and everything looks good. You must have been
delighted with Cork. Some reception you got. No letter
to-day but I suppose Cork and the excitement upset you
naturally — anyway I'll see you I hope on Friday.

Now good-bye dear. With fond love.

Yours,

Kit.

Hope you won't forget little piece *I* want for papers also.
Walsh is the devil: he sold them even the weekly *Sketch*.
Did you see Lady Lavery's picture of you in *The Sketch*.
Not you of course.[2] Helen is still with us, and Chrys is
coming on Saturday. How is Johnnie?

1. Alice Cooney's brother.
2. Lady Lavery's portrait of Collins in *The Sketch* of 8 March 1922
   is unbelievably bad. On the facing page there are three photographs
   of 'M. Collins's fiancée, Miss Kitty Kiernan'.

Letter 148

Mícheál, Dublin, to Kitty, 15 March 1922.

Kitty dearest,

Am just scribbling you a line at 10.30 Wednesday night.
Am going from the office now pretty straight to bed. Writing
this just so that you'll have some reminder from me on
St Patrick's Day, and I meant to get something for you but
really I hadn't time. However, I send you a sprig of shamrock
— a few leaves from a little bunch given me by some poor
children at a railway station as I returned from Cork. I
haven't anything else near me here that I can send.

You'll have my love and my thoughts as I go down in the
morning and I'm sure you won't be forgetful of me either —
that's not being too sure, is it?

Goodbye, Kitty dear, for a day or so. May try a note
on the train tomorrow. God be with you.

Fondest love always,
Mícheál.

Have you had any more outings? Keep them up. They'll be
great for you.

Letter 149

*Kitty, to Mícheál, Wednesday, received Saturday, 18 March
1922.*

My very dear Mícheál,

Picture my disgust last evening when my letter was late
for post. Was simply mad, as I wanted you to know that,
even tho' *I* didn't get a letter, I was writing. Was it not very
sad? I sent it, however, so you may get it to-morrow. Don't
understand your letter to-day saying you got no letter from
me. I wrote Friday and Saturday, also on Monday. Perhaps
Monday's note was also late for post. The most maddening
thing of all is when you write and it's late.

I hope you will have some little rest when you go to Cork
this time. Please *you* remember *me*, and do rest. In fact, in
the words of a great man: 'If you follow my advice you'll
always be right'.[1]

Glad to know I am before your mind. *That's very* satisfactory. Do you notice that I am not in a sentimental mood
these times? Did you ever feel that it could be an effort to be
so? Don't misunderstand me: I look upon this mood and
feeling as a good sign that I am getting well. I mean physically
stronger, because I know *I* would not be half so dependent
or silly if I felt my own self. Now it's not a case of the
carpenter quarrelling with his tools, or that I wish it had
been. No, I don't. It is just the weird thing that it should
affect me thus. No sentimental rot about you but a feeling
of confidence, and palship [*sic*]. No silly mean worries about
you but just that everything is all right. That is probably the
way you have been feeling, and hence I envied you.

Just imagine you are off to Cork [again] to-morrow. I am
off to Dublin without any worry or fear. I think it is just the

140

right thing, your duty to go to Cork, and my duty to go and have a good time. And yet we have a grand feeling that we can trust each other, knowing that if either of us offends we will pay the penalty sooner or later in remorse. Those things are paid back one day. I am not preaching, but it is satisfactory, for the one who doesn't offend, to know this.

To go back to to-morrow: Maud, Helen and *I* are going up to-morrow evening and staying at the Gresham for the dance on Friday night. I visit the doctor incidentally and, if he doesn't object, I'm going to dance in the Gresham on the 17th. I have a boy who is taking me all for myself. I know I'd get lots now to dance with me, because of Michael Collins and a job thrown in, but this dancing partner has always been my dancing partner. I suppose there will be talk of my dancing with him a lot but, when *you* don't object, I hope they talk about something new for a change. I may see Harry too, but trust me. By Saturday evening when you come back I'll be tired of everybody, and then will have *you* to amuse me. Did it ever strike you that you could amuse me? Don't think I am trying to make you feel small. You are too big to feel small.

It is funny. I started this letter with the idea it would be short and cool. I had no news or anything. It is a surprise to myself that it has turned out to be so long. And, as to it being cool, I'd rather be in one's heart in a cool manner, than gush in a way that would not last. 'Hot love soon cools' stile [*sic*] of thing! That was one of the things which, at the beginning of our romance, haunted me, that it might be a passing thing, not something genuine in keeping with my nature. . . .

Good bye my love 'till' Saturday. Don't be *too* nice to the Cork girls, and I'll not be too nice at the dance.
Bye bye again.

It's a long time till Saturday. I'm getting lonely.
Yours,
K. K.

Sent you a wire today, just to spite the ould post.

1. She may have been attempting a paraphrase of something by de Valera.

Letter 150

Mícheál, Dublin, to Kitty, 24 March 1922.

My own dearest Kitty,

This is a little note which you may not expect. It may be welcome to you in the morning. I hope so at any rate. Am writing it in that hope. Have just thought of doing it. It would be very funny, if you thought of the same thing.

It's very difficult to write a real letter in the circumstances, as I am looking forward to seeing you in fifteen minutes. So goodbye until then.

All my love,
Mícheál.

Letter 151

Kitty, to Mícheál, Saturday, received probably 27 March 1922.

My very dear Mícheál,

This will only be a note as I didn't get up till 11 o'c. Chrys, Maud, and I had a *tête à tête* in bed. Then I sent you a wire. 'Delighted'! You are delighted too. It was NOT so easy after all! I am as happy as possible, and I'll pray all the time for you now that all may be well.

I'll try to be better. I mean I'll try to understand and no more — 'little rows', was it?

Curse this uninteresting, drunken, letter.

Gearóid has just arrived, in great form; and Ducky if only you were here. I'd be so nice, and I do look so nice (some cheek!) to-day, free and happy, and I love you with the real real thing, and you know it. Yes, you do. I want you to know because you deserve it all, and you will see if I don't repay you. That's enough.

Will write a long one when I've recovered properly from all the dissipation, such as my forgetting to wire last night for car and nearly having to walk home. Love. Goodbye, my love.

Yours,
Kate.

Your letter today *was* a glorious surprise. Do you like this nice paper and the K?

Hugs and everything.

Letter 152

Kitty to Mícheál, Monday, received 28 March 1922.

My very dear Mícheál,

Was delighted to know from today's paper that you had such a good meeting in Waterford, not to speak of Dungarvan!

Gearóid said he thought you would be going to London tonight. If I knew your address for certain there I'd write. Suppose you won't get this until you return.

I am feeling much better, but I was looking and feeling very ill when I came back. I must never go to Dublin again, as it takes too much out of me, until I feel equal to it. Late nights and running about are not for me any longer. The doctor says in two months I'll be just perfect again if I follow his advice, and then I can 'Do *anything*'. So that's nice, and I'll look forward to that time.

I hope you are feeling well and sleeping. I was looking at G last night and just thinking how much better and fresher he looks than you and younger, even tho' he is older, isn't he?

What day can you come? Larry expects Harry here for the point-to-point on Thursday.

Excuse short note. I'll write more later. I hadn't to work at all to-day, Monday, because I looked ill!! So I read a book all day. Very nice to look ill sometimes.

Goodbye, dear.

> Fondest love.
> Yours,
> Kit.

I don't mean to appeal to your vanity when I refer to Gearóid. Nor am I finding fault. Only just thinking.

Letter 153

Kitty, to Mícheál, Wednesday, received 31 March 1922.

My very dear Mícheál,

Many thanks for letter received today. I was very sorry to know that you did have to go to London after all. I hope you will be able to get back soon, and I hope you get this alright.

Chrys is still here. She is going back on Friday, I think, but I don't think I'm going with her. I may go later on.

Glad to know you are calling on your way back from Castlebar. Are you motoring?

I enclose cheque. Thanks for paying my bill for me. Don't forget to send it if convenient, but if you have already done away with it, it's all right.

Good bye now.

Fondest love, Yours,
Kitty.

P.S. I was nearly forgetting to thank you for the lovely time you gave me in town, Joe etc.[1] It's not too late yet, is it?

1. Joe Hyland on whom Collins relied to drive him occasionally in Dublin. He carried a permit which enabled him to pass successfully through police and military cordons.

Letter 154

Kitty, to Mícheál, Tuesday, received on return from London, 1 April 1922.

My very dear Mícheál,

I got your Saturday's letter this morning, and on the second post I got yesterday's. Many thanks.

I'll be looking forward to seeing you at the weekend, I hope. Glad you were feeling well after your meetings, and glad that you don't have to go to London.

It's well I didn't write to the Jermyn Court Hotel, but I asked Gearóid to ask you to wire me your address in London on Monday if you were going for certain Monday night, as he seemed to have an idea you were going there. So when I didn't hear yesterday I didn't bother.

I am feeling better to-day, and have almost recovered from my late nights etc. in Dublin. Silly little fool I am to make myself so tired and weary by doing things that I shouldn't. I'll write you a long letter tomorrow, so forgive this scribble.

Good bye dear.

Fondest love, Yours,
Kit.

Am not forgetting cheque. Would you mind sending me that bill as part of it is Helen's and I want to send it to her.   K.

Mícheál tries to insist that Kitty should have a quiet holiday. She has agreed to go somewhere but can't make up her mind where. On 14 April, what has been called the first overt act of civil war occurs, the occupation in Dublin of the Four Courts, Fowler Hall in Parnell Square and the Kildare Street Club by what Collins calls 'the Rebel Army'. On that and subsequent days Mícheál once more takes Kitty to task for her failure to understand the circumstances in which he finds time to write to her at all. On 16 April when Griffith, escorted by Seán MacEoin and a contingent of the National Army, holds a meeting in Sligo despite an 'Irregular' proclamation, a car in which Collins is travelling back from Naas is attacked in a Dublin Street. The intention of the attackers, apparently, was to seize the car and were unaware of its occupants. A bullet, fired by one of them, narrowly missed Collins. Drawing a revolver he replied to the fire and, jumping from the car, caught the assailant in a doorway and held him prisoner. 'I see I was nearly losing you last night', Kitty says to him; Mícheál's comment is that 'God is better to us than we deserve.' From this time onwards attacks on the troops of the National Army and on positions occupied by them become an everyday affair. Kitty relays what she has heard from Harry Boland of de Valera's opinions of Griffith and Collins. She announces that on 30 April she will go to Bundoran for the long-promised rest.

Letter 155

Kitty, to Mícheál, Tuesday, received 5 April 1922.

My very dear Mícheál,

I hope you got back safely and that you were able to get to bed *early* (*my* early). I went to bed about 9 o'c and so had a good sleep, and am feeling better to-day.

I was delighted to see you again. As it was coming nearer and nearer to the time you might be here, it seemed *such* a length of time since I saw you, and I was never more glad to see you than when you did arrive. . . .

I hope your cold has gone, and I wish that I was near you to mind you. I love you all the more for coming from

Castlebar to see me, and I think I'd go the same length to
see you.

I'll let you know about the West when I've definitely
decided, but it will be the end of the week.

Goodbye. I'd write more only it's time for post. Will write
long ones later.

Your own little pet,
Kitty.

Excuse this short letter. The post goes one hour earlier now
(new time). That's why I couldn't write yesterday. Fondest
love, a hug and everything.

Your own Kit.

Letter 156

Mícheál, Dublin, to Kitty, 4 April 1922.

My own dearest Kitty,

Got back safely and I did go to bed early last night, not
perhaps so early as I might have gone but still before 12,
and that was really a feat, wasn't it? Feel much better this
morning, but still rather tired.

I want to tell you that I was really very very glad that I
had gone to Granard for I was scarcely ever so overjoyed
at seeing you — really and truly overjoyed although I was
not pleased with the way you were looking and I have been
thinking so much about you and the need for you to go
away. You will do what we said about that, won't you, and
you'll remain away for a month at least. I have got together
some books today — a list is enclosed. There is something of
interest in every one of them. Quite a lot about Longford
in *Rambles in Eirinn*,[1] and a very interesting lot too. Some
of them sound heavy, but they're not really. All the Talbot
Press ones were given to me by the shop. It strikes me
that I might send these on direct when you let me know
when exactly you are going and the address. Don't you think
this best? They make quite a good sized parcel. I'll get others
— of the novel class — also.

Am going off to a Dáil Cabinet meeting now and I'm
rushing as usual.

God be with you and I hope you'll soon be quite well
again and that we'll meet as arranged.

Fondest love,

Yours,

Mícheál.

1. *Rambles in Eirinn* by William Bulfin (Che Buono), first published in
   1907, ran into many impressions. There is a passing reference in it
   to Granard which Bulfin visited, and he quotes from a verse:
       And as I rode by Granard's moat,
       Right plainly might I see
       O'Ferrall's clans were sweeping down
       From distant Annaly.
   O'Ferrall's clans were 'sweeping down' to join the invading French,
   of course. See notes 2, 3, and 4 to Letter 25.

Letter 157

Kitty, to Mícheál, received 6 April 1922.

My very dear Mícheál,

I was delighted to get your letter to-day. I'll let you know
what day I am going. Perhaps I'll send you a wire. Don't send
the books until you know my address for certain as I haven't
decided where I'm going yet, but I'll know tomorrow
definitely.

Your letter to-day was lovely. I was delighted with it. Also
I'll be delighted to get the books. Glad you got to bed
before 12 o'c. If only you could do that for a while. I hope
you will be alright on Sunday. I hate the thought of those
meetings, but I'll pray for you.

I read *Rambles in Eirinn*, but am sure I could read it
again — as it's ages ago since I saw it.

I'll say bye bye now. With very fondest love and kisses
to my own lovie,

Your own, Kit.

Fr Malachy arrived home to-day. I haven't seen him yet!
Harry wrote to Larry saying he is coming tomorrow for a
hunt!

Excuse this short note — but you will, I know.

All my love to *You*.

Yours, K.

Letter 158

Kitty, to Mícheál, 6 April 1922, received 7 April 1922.

My very dear Mícheál,

Haven't gone yet. The lady I was to have gone to is coming to Nobber[1] for Easter, so I can't go to her until Easter week. Disappointing isn't it? I may go to Gowna for a few days at the end of this week or beginning of next, so you can keep the books for a few weeks more! Don't be vexed with me. The fates seem to be against my departure.

Thanks for letter to-day. I hope you are well and sleeping, and I hope I'll see you soon again. I'll let you know when I am leaving here. Feeling better to-day, but disgusted about Connemara. But sure it can't be helped. I heard only yesterday evening that the lady had arranged to come to Meath for Easter.

I send you my best love, and a big hug and kiss.

Lovingly Yours,
Kitty.

1. Nobber, near Kells, Co. Meath.

Letter 159

Mícheál, Dublin, to Kitty, 10 April 1922.

My dearest Kitty,

No letter again today. I got back from Wexford late last night but it was only this morning I got your wire. There was a very good meeting at Wexford and a very good reception all along both going and coming. No interruption at all at the meeting.

What has happened to you — though seriously — not to have written for three days? I suppose you've been enjoying yourself too well or something — staying up all night and in bed at day. Is that it? How did the hunt go on? Honestly I do think it's a shame you haven't written. But then I may be hard on you, and there may be a *real* reason, and if I said anything — but then I don't say *any things* that I have to regret afterwards.

148

Things are rapidly becoming as bad as they can be, and
the country has before it what may be the worst period
yet. A few madmen may do anything. Indeed they are
just getting on the pressure gradually — they go on from
cutting a tree to cutting a railway line, then to firing at
a barrack, then to firing at a lorry, and so on. But God
knows I do not want to be worrying you with these things.

Are you going to Nobber for Easter? Or are you going
anywhere? I'm most awfully anxious to see you *quickly*
and this week is going to be a bad week with me by the
look of things. Any improvement in the Connemara
plans yet? Kitty, do please hurry up making that definite,
but I am anxious about you. I wonder if you're writing even
today — Yes? No?

May God bless you.

> Fondest love,
> Mícheál.

Letter 160

Kitty, to Mícheál, Monday, received 11 April 1922.

My dear sweetheart,

I hope you will excuse me for not writing for the last few
days, but I was away two days. Hope you got my wire on
Saturday. I told Miss Keneghan to send it about 11 o'c. Had
she done so it would have been handed in same time as you
sent yours to me.

I hope you are well after Wexford and that your cold has
gone. G[earóid] was home yesterday and last evening. I was
wishing to myself that you were here.

I'll tell you all about H[arry] when I see you. He went off
on the 6 o'c on Saturday. He had a great hunt on Friday.

Maud is going away for a few days around Easter. So I'll
not get away for a long holiday until she returns. When will
you come again? And what about a holiday for you?

We are going to Longford races tomorrow. Wish you would
be there.

Bye bye. Fondest love to Ducky.

> Your own
> Kit.

Letter 161

Kitty, to Mícheál, Wednesday, received Thursday 12 April 1922.

My own dear sweetheart,

I was very sorry last night that I came away before the
'phone was free for us. It was getting late and the others were
anxious to get home. I'd love to know if you tried to get me
any more or what happened. I went off about a half-hour
from the time you sent me away. It was the devil to hear, and
me just dying to talk to you and *a* voice *all* the time saying
'Please let me speak to Seán McKeon', but you settled that.

Well how are you? I am *most* anxious to see you. If you
can't come for even a night before Sunday, then do come on
Sunday evening. For a few days now I am anxious to see
you and it's years and years since we met and indeed your
voice yesterday made me ever more longing to be near you.
So do come soon. Ah do!

Got your letter last night and your letter this morning.
Such a cheery surprise your letter this morning, because you
never told me yesterday that you had written. But you
are a dote, my dote, and nobody else's. And your little pet
sends love, a hug and a big big kiss and she wants you to
excuse this lovely writing but it's time to post it.

> Your own.
> All my love even if I miss post
> by sending it,
> Kit.

Letter 162

Kitty, to Mícheál, received 14 April 1922.

My very dear Mícheál,

At last I have 'almost' decided — and I'll go next week
sometime. It may be Bundoran after all, as it is milder than
Connemara which is forty miles from anywhere, and I'd
be very lonely there. So I'll go to Bundoran first. It is lovely
and quiet there too, but not so out of the way. I think I'd
die in Connemara, so far from everyone.

I am looking forward to Sunday. If you can't come, send
me a wire so that I'll know and not be so disappointed!
But you will come, please the Lord, and perhaps you might
stay a while with your country friends!

I spent part of the day in the garden to-day with a nice
book, *Lysbeth* by Rider Haggard. So I feel fine. I'll be A.1.
when I get to Bundoran. I was there before, so I know what
it's like. Whereas I don't know Connemara — and being forty
miles away I'd have to stay a while if I went. Do you agree
with me?

I had a note from Harry a few days ago. Larry expects
him next week, I hear!

And how is poor old Ducky? Killed writing me wonderful
love letters, like the one I got to-day, in fact every day. They
are certainly most wonderful from the point of view of love!
See if Ducky can't write a love one for a change. Tell him
I said so. Now don't forget, and love and love and love and
_____ from Me.

I send you an Easter Egg of a hug. [She attempts a picture.]
Sorry can't draw or you might get more eggs.

Letter 163

Mícheál, Dublin, to Kitty, 14 April 1922.

My own dearest Kitty,

It's all very well for you to find fault with my letters. If
you could only see the circumstances under which most of
them are written, you wouldn't be so mighty quick to
disparage them. At any rate I won't mind you this time.

The 'almost' decided is good too — honestly do decide
quickly. I'm worrying about it — I am really — and let it be
whatever place you like. I was never in Bundoran, so I can't
say what it's like, but I fancy it's rather nice. Hope it's not
going to be a kind of miniature Dublin. You know what I
mean. It sounds more like a holiday place than a resting
place, but any place at all for a change of air and scene etc.
Will you let me know when you are actually going? Of course
I can never be sure until you're positively there.

We did nothing at the Conference yesterday — except talk,

talk all the time — it's simply awful. And the country! But *they* never think of the country at all — they only think of finding favour for their own theories, they only think of getting their own particular little scheme accepted.

I very sincerely trust you'll find this letter a bit more acceptable than the others. I'll wire tomorrow. They're planning some kind of a performance for Naas tomorrow night, but I may be able to get out of it. G[earóid] will be with me and that may help.

All the nice parts and messages of my letters are at the beginning and ending

May God be with you.

Fondest love, Mícheál.

The Rebel Army has taken over the Four Courts. God help them! M.

Letter 164

Kitty, to Mícheál, Friday, received 15 April 1922.

Dearest Mícheál,

I don't know if there are any mails going out this evening but am chancing writing at any rate. It is raining here at a terrific rate all day, so I didn't go out yet.

Did you visit Mrs McL[1] yet? I'll make no comment just now. I might say too much. Her remark about me was as doubtful a compliment as the one you paid me. I prayed for you yesterday evening when in the church which I visited three times. Amongst other things I prayed that you might be able to avoid people of her type. Now, don't be vexed with me. I can't help thinking sometimes, and that particular thing hurts *me* more than anything else. So can you blame me?

I hope you will be able to manage to come on Sunday, and I do hope you are feeling well and sleeping. Now bye bye.

Fondest love,
from Kitty.

1. She obviously did not like Mrs McLaverty, possibly seeing in her a rival. See Letter 191. Mrs McLaverty was the wife of a leading Dublin gynaecologist.

Letter 165

Mícheál, Dublin, to Kitty, 15 April 1922, telegram.

Thanks for letter this morning. Appreciate very much what
you say about person referred to. Sorry I can't possibly leave
town owing to the situation here. May not go to meeting.
With love,

Mícheál.

Letter 166

Kitty to Mícheál, Monday, received Tuesday 18 April 1922.

My very dear Mícheál,
    I see I was very nearly losing you last night. Why didn't
you come to Granard from Naas? Even when I got your wire
on Saturday evening, saying you mightn't get going to Naas,
I *knew* you'd go.
    Did you get my wire and love message on Saturday evening?
There was no post here to-day so I don't know if you wrote
to me on Saturday.
    I believe H[arry] is coming to-night for a hunt to-morrow!
Maud is going to town this week for a few days holidays
with G[earóid] somewhere. We see G. very often here now.
He was to have called last Thursday.
    Rushing for post so good-bye dear.

Best love,
Yours,
K.

Letter 167

Mícheál, Dublin, to Kitty, 18 April 1922, part of letter.

My own dearest Kitty,
    Your letter came to hand this morning — I was very glad
indeed to get it. Sent you a wire yesterday evening but I'm
afraid it did not go last night. It was delayed by the lad who
took it. I thought it well to send you a message to reassure
you, but you knew I'd be all right, didn't you? God is better
to us than we deserve.

I have just come back from the funeral of poor Frank
Lawless.[1] It's awfully sad about him. He was one of the
decentest men in the Dáil. Killed accidentally. No one to
say that he died for the Free State or for the Republic —
and that's the way.

Honestly I did not know that I was going to Naas. I
thought things might have been much worse here, but they
turned out all right and so I was able to go. It was immediately
after our return the shooting took place. I think they must
have meant to capture me only. They were great optimists.
God help them, but they are carrying things a bit too far.

When are you going . . .

1. One of the early Volunteer commandants who took part in the
   1916 Rising, and was imprisoned until June 1917; he was a member
   of the Second Dáil and supported the Treaty.

Letter 168

Mícheál, Dublin, to Kitty, 19 April 1922.

My own dearest Kit,

No letter from you this morning — that's not nice of
you. I expect it's a kind of retaliation, but it isn't fair.
Perhaps, however, you have gone away, although I fear
that isn't the case. And here I am writing to you just the
same. And I'm writing before 9.30 and that's a time you
were only up at twice in your life except when you stayed
up all night — and that's that.

I have nothing to say this morning except to repeat
what I said yesterday, that I'm very anxious to see you.
It seems about a million years since we met and that's a
long time, and really and truly I'm rather going off work
thinking of you, and that's not a very good thing either.
I wonder if you'd come to Dublin for a day or two days
before going to Bundoran. This isn't anything in the nature
of orders — see how meek I'm becoming. Will you dear
dear Kitty?

That's all this time. No more letters until you've written
four at least.

God be with you.

Fondest love, Mícheál.

154

Letter 169

Kitty, to Mícheál, Wednesday, received 20 April 1922.

My very dear Mícheál,

I was delighted to get your long letter to-day. You had nearly beaten me. Saturday, Sunday, Monday, without writing. I was about to write to you yesterday when some people called. I am all alone here to-day. Maud and Larry went to town. Larry is taking home the car to-morrow night, and Mops may go to Greystones for a few days' holidays, so I won't be able to go to Bundoran until next week probably. I am sorry to disappoint *you*, but we can't be away very well together, and the weather may be finer next week, and so better for Bundoran as it's a very open sea. You make a mistake if you think Bundoran a miniature Dublin. It's deadly dull, and I wonder if I'll survive there, but I'll give it a trial anyway.

Pity Greystones is so near Dublin and so crowded as it's ideal otherwise. Delighted you had even a few hours there. I like to hear of you having even a short time in such a place. It sounds more normal. If you went sufficiently to places of that sort and met that kind of people, you would never have asked me to marry you. I mean this not as a reflection on you, but upon myself. It is not very pleasant for me to feel like that, but I often do, but lack the courage to tell you so when I meet you and am carried away. It is strange that I feel all right and confident when I'm with you, but once you are gone. . . . Now please don't misunderstand me. I am not telling you this to make you unhappy, but just to be straight with myself and you.

Glad Mrs Doyle isn't annoyed with me as I owe her a letter for ever ever so long. Yes, she *is* sweet. I always thought so, and Mrs Barniville is sweet-looking too, and I am sure very nice if one knew her.

Yes, the shooting was a bit exciting for me, perhaps a bit too much so, for my present condition. Yes, God is indeed good, extraordinarily good to you.

Perhaps you would like to come tomorrow evening for the night, providing, of course, that you might be able to steal a few hours off — or perhaps motor with Larry, but the journey is long and cold at night even tho' the inclination might be strong. A day like this would be just perfect for motoring, but the days get so cold just yet, so the train might be better. If you can come, send a wire early: if you can't, I'll understand and forgive you! Nice of me! Now bye bye, dear, and my fondest love.

Yours,
Kit.

I am feeling better every day T.G., and having now a large bottle of stout every day! So I'll get fat.

It was sad about poor Mr Lawless. Is Mr Murphy that I met in the Shelbourne dead? I saw where a Mr Murphy from Buffalo died with Archdeacon to his name.[1]

I got your wire on Monday evening. I was expecting it all day! I send you my love and everything as usual. Isn't this a long letter? Yours was very nice to-day. You were great to follow the man on Sunday night and to catch him.

K.

1. John Archdeacon Murphy, referred to here, was a native of Buffalo who in August 1916, was sent to Ireland by Clan na Gael, the American counterpart of the IRB, with a large sum of money for prisoners' dependents. He was also interested in recreating the republican movement in Ireland after the Easter débâcle.

Letter 170

Mícheál, Dublin, to Kitty, 20 April 1922.

My dearest Kitty,

It was time you wrote — honestly it was. But I was glad to get your letter even though there were some very unpleasant things in it. There were you know. And it's not fair of you to be talking like you do about certain things not happening if I saw more of other people. You must know in your heart it isn't so. And it's not a nice thing to retaliate in that way just because I say a few nice things about friends of *your own*. But it's because you're in bad form. And that's that!

And now about Bundoran: you're awful, positively awful! Put off again! What do you think of that idea of mine about coming up for a few days before you go there? Wouldn't that suit Greystones, and as you're travelling at all the journey here won't be so much extra. What do you say? Please do it, but I'll leave it to yourself.

There will be no chance that I can go down tomorrow night as I have to leave on the morning train on Saturday for Tralee and Killarney. Then I won't be back until Monday evening. I've had every Sunday at it now since the Dublin meeting, and it's becoming very wearying, but maybe we'll have a rest soon.

Haven't been able to get your little gold watch yet. I send for it religiously two or three times a week. I think I told you they had to send it to England.[1]

May God be with you, and do take care of yourself.

Fondest love,
Mícheál.

1. See Letter 121.

Letter 171

Kitty to Mícheál, Thursday, received 21 April 1922.

My own Mícheál,

It is 5.30 and, in case you may not be able to come to-night, I'm writing so as you won't be disappointed in the morning. Wires take hours to get here.

I was delighted with your letter to-day. It *was* a nice one — really and truly as you say — and I, of course, was full of remorse for what I said in mine yesterday but with me those little feelings are only passing things, so in that way you excuse me, don't you? I wanted to — or could have — put my two arms round your neck this morning and give you a real big hug, the sort of one I used to love to give you, and that *used* to make me tired, I used to do it with such violence. It has often struck me since that they musn't have been at all pleasant for the *One* receiving them! Of course they *were* meant to be nice.

I was in bed when your letter came, and I had a *great* conversation with you. You would have laughed.

Have you seen Mops? I had a wire from Larry to-day
to attend a funeral, which I've just done, so I'm a useful
sort of creature.

> Bestest love to you.
> Your own.
> Kit.

Letter 172

Kitty, to Mícheál, Friday, received 25 April 1922.

My very dear Mícheál,

I am in great form to-day for a change, you'll be glad
to know. Of course I expected you last night, but find that
in your letter this morning you say you can't come tonight.
How funny. I never even suggested tonight. I'd be too wise
or knowing to suggest *that*. With *Saturday* following Friday,
you would have to go off on some train, car or other
to Tralee or around.

I had a list of your meetings in my mind from the night
I last left Dublin. I read them in the train in an evening paper.
Ever since I could have told you where you had intended
speaking *etc*! Very clever of me, isn't it? Oh no, I'd never
invite you to Granard on the eve of a big meeting. I mean
on the eve of your departing for a big meeting so far away
as Tralee where you must go the day before. Read my letter.
I said or at least meant last night, Thursday.

Larry was to have brought home the car. He wired he was
coming yesterday, but only got here this morning. Car wasn't
ready, so he came by train. You would have had an excellent
excuse, Ducky, no Larry no car. Pity you didn't know. I'd
have great satisfaction believing you couldn't get to him or
something. But Larry says he never even saw you.

Anyway, to make this long story short, I was expecting
you last night, and never for a long time was I *so* disappointed
about anything. The feeling was awful while it lasted. I had
nothing to go on. Yet I can't tell why I should have
expected you, only that I built a little castle in the air,
that you'd see Larry go away in the car from the Gresham,
and be tempted to come with him, to give me a surprise
without wiring. But I'd be kind of ready to greet you, so it

wouldn't be such a little surprise as you had imagined, and I could smile to myself. Now haven't I a good imagination to have expected all this?

I went for a walk with Paul and talked the feeling off. We talked of everything under the sun, including what fools Irishmen are to give up everything for their country.

I *wanted* to see you. I was looking well and feeling well, which is still better. I am eating everything that's good, and trying to be good in this way, so that if I go on I'll be a big fat lump (an expression of mine always when I want to think of something huge). And I wanted to show you a few things of no importance really but just to get your opinion while here.

Have you seen Mops? I had to smile when you suggested my going to town, as I had intended, or rather have to go for just one day next week before I go north. And really and truly, I'd rather go for the day, and be unattached for just one day, so as I could get doing my work and concentrate on *it*. Then when I got to the train for home, I could feel that no one would say to Joe McGuinness (T.D.), 'Oh she lives in Dublin, only goes home for week-ends.' I have always, all my life, gone there, and always hope to.

You are not the *only* attraction there, dear. What I mean is that Dublin suits me in many ways, and you are the only attraction when that's over. But that's a different thing. I mean if you were not living there, I'd be still there. But, of course, now I'll see you we can arrange that, but it will be the middle of next week.

Rushing for post. Have had several interruptions.

My fondest love. Always your own loving,

Kit.

Letter 173

Kitty, to Mícheál, Tuesday, received 5 o'clock, Wednesday, 26 April 1922.

My very dear Mícheál,

There was no post here yesterday, so I couldn't write.

Glad to see by to-day's paper that you had such good meetings down South. When did you get back?

159

I thought you would send a wire. The papers don't come in here till 1 o'c. new time, but I saw the *Sunday Independent* yesterday and it didn't look very cheery about Saturday's meeting. So I was 'wondering' how you would do on Sunday, or would yourself and Seán be shot!

Mops didn't come back yet and she never wrote, so I don't know where she is. She is paying me back, because I never wrote when in Dublin. She and George were to have gone to Punchestown[1] to-day. Some swank!

Did you get my Friday letter on Saturday? You were to have gone on Saturday morning, but I imagine you didn't go till noon, so I expect you got my letter all right. You never write on Saturday. Neither do I. We had a great holiday here yesterday, but it was a sad one for me.

I see Dev is still at it. Last time H[arry] was here he told me (in a burst of confidence) of Dev's dislike for you, because you were too anxious for power, that Dev liked Griffith, but Harry dislikes Griffith, and (of course) likes you, etc.

Harry didn't come last week. I think it was Larry's fault tho'. He wrote to Larry saying he'd like to come to another hunt, and for Larry to wire him. Larry did, but very late, but was with him since in town. He wrote me but I didn't reply yet.

I may go to town on Friday for a day to the dentist etc. Then I have to go to Bundoran on Saturday, D.V.

And now I'll finish.

With fond love,
Yours,
K.

Was in the middle of a long confab. with you in Friday's letter when I was interrupted badly by a lad Larry left me to give a hand to, so I had to switch off. It was a queer ending to what might have been an interesting letter. That's the way.

Write soon.

P.S. Excuse blots and dirt.

1. A stylish racing occasion.

Letter 174

Kitty, to Mícheál, Friday, in pencil, received 1 May 1922.

Mícheál,

I apologise for that letter I wrote but I couldn't help writing it. I felt so bitter because I am ill. It is only since last summer. Before then I was never a day ill in my life.

I am very little use to you in my present condition, and only wish that you found someone big and strong to love you.

I am not leaving here 'till next week, perhaps Monday.

Maud is back. She has got her ring. It is a beauty. G[earóid] wired to-day. He didn't see her off last evening, and she says he had a note from you for me.

Got your letter to-day. Very nice of you to be thinking of me, and to be 'a kind of very lonely'. Hope you are A.1.

Love.
Yours,
Kit.

In May there are only two letters and a telegram of Kitty's, and a mere handful of Mícheál's. She is ill and writes strange letters. She spends some time in the Grand Hotel, Greystones, where Mícheál sees her frequently in the late evenings, making letter-writing of course unnecessary. Towards the end of the month he travels to London to discuss the British reaction to his 'democratic' Constitution — they see it as 'a Republic under the thinnest of disguises' — and to hear their criticisms of his failure to establish the authority of the Provisional Government. He wants arms for the National Army which, striving against all the odds, he fears may have to be used against the Four Courts and the other places occupied by the Irregulars. The British are reluctant to give him what he wants. Their forces in the country are not immune from attack. Some more soldiers have been killed, and a naval tug seized. At the back of their minds the British are fearful that, if their forces are completely withdrawn, the Treaty will go by default, and that they will be forced militarily to reestablish their position in the whole of Ireland, including the North where Sir Henry Wilson, the former Commander of the Imperial General Staff, is now the adviser to the Minister of Home Affairs on the organisation and conduct of the Special Constabulary.

Collins's position is incredibly difficult. While keeping a reconciling eye on the various anti-Treaty groupings he feels constrained, in order to ensure a free general election, to enter into a pact with de Valera, now leader of Cumann na Poblachta. This provided that a panel of candidates, representing the existing division in the Dáil and in Sinn Féin, would together enter the election and afterwards share an executive of five ministers from whichever party obtained a majority and four from the minority. The British disliked this pact, as indeed Griffith did, and its existence did not make the discussions in London on the constitution any easier for Collins. 'Collins was in a most pugnacious mood', the civil servant Jones (p.203) recorded on 27 May, 'and his first sentence to me was "The gulf is unbridgeable". He talked on at a great rate in a picturesque way about going back to fight alongside his comrades Mulcahy and Mac Keown [sic] . . . I communicated my anxiety about Collins to the P.M. and concealed nothing of the belligerent mood of Collins and the silence of Griffith. The P.M. said it looked like a break.' A little of this atmosphere is conveyed in Collins's letters to Kitty.

Letter 175

Kitty, to Mícheál, 22 May 1922, telegram.

Going town this evening. Will arrive 6.20.

K.

Letter 176

Kitty to Mícheál, Monday, no indication when received.

My very dear Mícheál,
    I was very disappointed to-day. No letter from you.

Perhaps the one you said you were writing on Sunday will
come to-morrow. I got your wire on yesterday morning —
suppose it was sent late on Saturday evening. How are
you since? I expect very busy.

Nothing strange here. We went to Omard yesterday and
played tennis between the showers.

The hotel is nearly finished now. We may go into it the
end of this week. The range has been keeping us back so
far — no breakfast in bed if we went there. There is a holiday
on Thursday next,[1] perhaps you might come down then.
Will you? It is a long time since you were here.

I have been thinking of you (sensibly) quite a lot since
the last time I saw you, sometimes very happy and
sometimes sad, and then trying to analyse myself, and I think
there is a good deal in what you say about me, but I do think
I am a bit of an extremist as regards my liking for you. I'm
either wonderfully great with you, or wonderfully out with
you. Now I am sure if I had 200 years to live, the first 100
would be spent in the extreme, but I'd find in the second
100 I'd be able to strike the happy medium, and of course
be far far happier. I find what's wrong with me now (and
perhaps with you) is that I can't find the medium. Then I
console myself by thinking that, after all, I am amateurish in
my love. I feel just like a little child who is only beginning to
learn something — as there is a lot to learn in love, if it is to
be a success. I know I have made a bad attempt even for a
beginner, but I was always a bad beginner in everything, so
that's no surprise to me, and all the time, since I really loved
you, I know I am making childish mistakes, always childish
I find. I get little disappointments and things, and find that
love isn't all sunshine. And then I am unpractical. I close my
eyes deliberately to the other side, which I do believe is
the interesting side in life.

You say there is a lot of good in me. Sometimes I think
there is, but it is so hidden and far away. It may be because
the most of my life I've never been allowed to think for
myself, and nobody to take a decent interest in me. The best
was then kept back but, thank God, I had always the brains
to realize if only I got a chance. For the past six years I had
more of my own way and I proved to myself what was in me

163

and I was ever so happy and could make others happy, too —
but I never met anyone that I was willing to give myself to
although forced (as perhaps very few have been) but I always
held out and I marvel how I did it.

Men interested me to a certain extent. The more I
associated with them the more I appreciated myself,
although sometimes I tried to fool myself, especially with
that boy Lionel after the burning [of the hotel]. I felt
perhaps I'd have to go off and work. He was extremely
wealthy and loved me. I tried to picture marrying him. But
I was beyond him. He couldn't understand me. I tried and
tried to come down to his level. He had no brains. He was
polite beyond words. It got on my nerves. He was so
thoughtful to everyone as well as me. You know the type,
jumping up and down when people came into the room.
No one recognised Kitty when he was about. I tried so hard
to be just ordinary when he was here, but he still used to feel
uncomfortable. Then he'd go away, and write. How extraordinary and wonderful I seemed, that he could not
understand me, but that I was too good for him etc. He made
a hopeless attempt. I was his first — and I was one year older
than he was (he didn't know this, *that* also was funny). I
tried to be sensible about him because he was young and a
good boy and very manly in a way, but any way I remember
always wishing he was different. I suppose wishing he was
you or someone like you — I didn't know you then. To make
a long story short, poor Lionel will never believe in women
again after I promising to marry him (always a perhaps tho').

Have written this in shop, so excuse. Sorry I haven't time
to write more this time. You can never say I don't write
long letters.

Love from
Kit.

I suppose you won't be able to make head or tail of this
letter or know what it's all about, as I don't myself. Anyway,
if you are not busy, you'll read it!

Love,
Kit.

1. It has not been possible to fix the date of this letter. There were
three possible (Church) holidays on a Thursday in May-June 1922.

Letter 177

Mícheál, s.s. Cambria, *to Kitty, 26 May 1922.*

My own dearest Kitty,

   I am writing this on the boat — the others have left my cabin and I am thus alone — and I sat thinking for a little while and then began to write this. Have a little vision of you before my mind's eye as you passed down the pier — this was prior to your seeing me and turning back. It was very pleasant to look at but it was lonely for me, and I thought of how lonely it must have been for you also. More lonely for you as you will have more time to think. And then I might have been so much nicer to you during those last moments — and I needn't find fault with some of those little things, need I? But I was preoccupied with the things which I am coming across to face. It's not easy, and then it's always those who are nearest to me suffer most and have to put up with most at my hands — and that's that!

   I wonder if this letter will really reach Granard tomorrow? And if it does, will you go yourself? Honestly I am looking forward to seeing you in town on Monday, but then perhaps I shan't be back at all on Monday. So many perhaps's.

   And now we are going on for Holyhead and I'm thinking very much of you, and of your visit to the doctor. You'll let me know how you got on.

   May God be with you always. My fondest love,
                                            Mícheál.

Letter 178

Mícheál, New Metropole Hotel, London, to Kitty, possibly 28 May 1922.

My dearest Kitty,

   I got your wire safely late last night — indeed I didn't expect it. But it was very pleasant to get it.

   Things are serious — far far more serious than any one at home thinks. In fact it is not too much to say that they are as serious as they were at the worst stage of the negotiations last year. And even while we are here there comes the news of two British soldiers being killed in Dublin and two ex-

policemen in Boyle. Coming at such a time it is impossible
to get away from the conclusion that they are done
deliberately to make things more difficult for us in our task
here. It is not very creditable to those who are responsible
for the actions themselves but it is simply disastrous for the
name of Ireland.

You ought to have seen some of the papers here
yesterday — M. Collins in Downing St with his sweetheart.
I can have all sorts of lovely libel actions. The Laverys took
me there in their car.[1] Some of the correspondents
recognised my friend but the story was too good! I must
bring you back some of the papers to show you.

Am writing this in the midst of a very worrying time.
But I mustn't make you worry. I wish you were here. I'll
never forget Greystones. It was lovely and I shouldn't like
to think of being there now unless you are still there. Perhaps
you are.

I am not returning until Tuesday morning — if I can even
then.

God be with you.

All my love, Mícheál.

1. See Letter 191 and note.

Letter 179

*Mícheál, New Metropole Hotel, London, to Kitty, 30 May
1922.*

My own dearest Kitty,
Am just scribbling a very very hurried line — at the
moment I don't know whether or not I shall be able to get
back tonight. Things are bad beyond words, and I am almost
without hope of being able to do anything of permanent
use. It's really awful — to think of what I have to endure here
owing to the way things are done by the opponents at home.

In any case, home or no home, I want to see you on
Saturday, and that's that for the moment. I'll let you know
exact time of travelling as soon as I can. How are you?

No letter at all from you.

God be with you.
Fondest love, M.

Letter 180

Mícheál, New Metropole Hotel, London, to Kitty, 31 May 1922.

My own dearest Kitty,

Still no word from you — perhaps you have written to Dublin and they have not forwarded your letters. At any rate I am returning tonight, and I shall see you with God's help on Saturday. The weather is awful here and everything is awful. I wish to God someone else was in the position and not I. But that's that.

It's almost heartbreaking not to have heard a word from you and I feel somehow or other that you're not thinking of me — but that's not it, is it?

Anyway unless you forbid it, I'll see you on Saturday. May God bless you.

> Fondest love,
> M.

———————————

Kitty, 'looking well and feeling well' after the restful days in Greystones, resumes her letter-writing in June. All the communications in that month, with the exception of a few letters and telegrams, are from her.

The trouble about the draft Constitution carried over into June and the British, extremely perturbed, examined what military, economic and financial measures were open to them if the dispute could not be settled harmoniously. The trouble on the Border continued ominously. The British looked askance at Collins: negotiating with him was compared to writing on shallow and agitated water. The line he was pursuing was one which his own colleagues did not believe could be maintained either. Ultimately he had to give way and leave the arguing of the case to those who felt more comfortable with the provisions of Treaty: Griffith and Kevin O'Higgins. The details were finally settled on 8 June by Hugh Kennedy, the Irish law officer, in consultation with the English lord chief justice, Lord Hewart. The agreed Constitution was published on 16 June, the day of the Irish general election. One consequence was the abandonment of the pact with de Valera; another was that confrontation with the armed anti-Treaty elements could not be deferred for much longer. Indeed, following a series of provocative acts, the army of the Provisional Government moved on 28 June to repossess the Four Courts and the other occupied buildings in Dublin city. In one of the engagements Cathal Brugha was killed, and the Gresham and Granville Hotels in O'Connell Street were burned to the ground. A 'national call to arms' was then issued, and a war council was formed by the Provisional Government with Collins as Commander-in-Chief. From headquarters in Portobello Barracks, he tackled the problem of suppressing armed opposition with determination and drive, and within six weeks had regained Waterford, Sligo, Limerick, Tuam, Tipperary, Cahir, Cashel, Clonmel and Dundalk. On 11 August the national troops entered Cork City from the sea, having earlier taken Tralee and Westport in similar manner. The letters reflect the current tensions. They indicate the strained conditions in which Collins is now living, as well as Kitty's growing anxiety.

Letter 181

Kitty, to Mícheál, Monday, received 2 June 1922.

My own dear Mícheál,

I got back safely on Saturday evening. Mops met me at the station and handed me your letter.

It was just like you to give me such a nice surprise. I'll write a long long letter and tell you all about it.

You will, dear sweetheart, forgive me writing this short note, but I'll explain when writing later.

I hope you are well and happy and that you know how happy I feel about my love for you and how much I look forward to the future with you.

This is a poor attempt at a letter but there are people here talking around me and asking me questions.

I got on fine with the doctor.

My love to you and every good wish. Good luck.

Yours,
Kit.

Of course I am very lonely.

Letter 182

Kitty, to Mícheál, 30 May 1922.

My very dear Mícheál,

I hope you were not disappointed with my short note of yesterday. I'll start now at where you and I left off on Friday evening. I said I'd write on Friday night but I didn't realise the hour it was; when I left the doctor it was 12 o'c.

When I came back to the Gresham on Friday evening I there and then decided not to go to your missioner and, as I had a few hours to spare, I went off to Confession. I got on *great*. I'll tell you about that some other time. It was rather funny. Anyway I came out of the Church feeling very happy. Then I met Larry and then went off to the doctor. I was only kept 2 hours! Dev called or something. The doctor was pleased with my looks, but tried to get me to stay on at Greystones. He thought it was the ideal place for me. Neither too bracing or relaxing etc etc.

Joe[1] took me back to Greystones, and there I found Gearóid and a few of the boys. The missioner had been there waiting for me but I returned too late, and he left. I didn't get to bed then until about 2 o'c. So the following day, Saturday, I was tired and only got up at 12 o'c, packed my belongings, said the good byes, and a special one for No. 7. Poor old No. 7! I think it was the room I liked best after all (don't ask all what as I am not there to reply.)

I went in to town at 6 o'c. Miss McD[2] is really a good sort and loves you. She never tires of talking about you. Miss Meany[3] is back. Miss Mc[4] was, I think, lonely after me. Don't know about Mrs O'C.[5]

Tom, Larry and Paul travelled home with me. Joe took me in from Greystones and took us all to the station and did some shopping for me at the station. We met Tom Barry with his wife,[6] and some of the Prices[7] were introduced to all. Barry was travelling to Sligo and was in our carriage. He was going to Donegal from Sligo. He and I seemed to hit it off well. He would like to have the 'pleasure' of showing me the West, I think, and Cork, and he made a few other nice remarks. I had some carnations Miss McD gave me, so I gave him one. He put it in his pocket book and, when he meets

169

me again, he'll have it! In fact he's coming here, perhaps
on his way back, and will stay. So now, what do you think
of that? I couldn't think from Adam if he was a friend of
yours or, if you liked him, as I never heard you speak much
of him. But I was diplomatic and said nothing, and then he
said 'won't we be some kind of cousins?' I said I hope so.
Was that right? We had a bit of fun in the train together,
and it passed the time when we were a few.

Mops met us at the station; she wasn't in too bad form.
I met Boland, McDonagh's partner.[8] He was telling me Joe
[McDonagh] had gone to USA on business for the Crokers.[9]

We went to Omard on Sunday and played tennis. Before
going, two men from Bangor called and I had to entertain
them, so please don't be vexed because I didn't write, and
there is no post on Sundays. I was very lonely thinking of
you all the time wondering how you would do in London.
When I left you on the boat I felt awful to think we had
really parted for the first time for nearly a month, and I
had the queerest feeling in the little cabin that I should be
with you and that the second bed was mine. *You* know the
feeling. I had a longing to please you and to make you
happy just there at that time, and I knew you were worrying
or preoccupied. And the missioner, only *you* could have
kept me from going to him, and now I'm glad I took your
advice. I'll try and go to confession every week for a while.
I shall never forget Greystones either, it was so restful and
happy. I could have done with a year of it with you near.
It was hard to tear myself away when the last day came,
the associations and recollections were so good. It was surely
a little bit of Heaven, now wasn't it, Ducky? I close my eyes
sometimes and think I can hear somebody say 'my wife'.

The hotel is not quite ready yet, but it's doing well. They
had a strike here and that kept it back. They all think here
that I look well, and I'm feeling well and thinking of you
and the time_____.

I got two letters from you to-day. I hope you will bring
back good news. I'd send this to London only I'm afraid
you would have gone. Don't forget to keep papers about
your sweetheart. It was extraordinary, wasn't it? I'd like to
see the papers. So don't forget.

Be sure to manage Saturday, if you can.
Bye bye my pet, my lovie and everything.
All my love to you.

Your devoted,
Kit.

In haste 'cuse.

1. Joe Hyland. See Letter 153.
2. Miss McDermott. See Letter 50, note 1.
3. Miss Meany, not identified.
4. Possibly Miss McCarthy of 44 Mountjoy St. See Letter 139, note 1.
5. Mrs Batt O'Connor? See Letter 50, note 2.
6. Tom Barry, the noted leader of a flying column in West Cork, and his wife Leslie Price.
7. The Prices had given distinguished service during the War of Independence, but the family divided over the Treaty. One of them, Eamonn, had been director of organisation on the headquarters staff of the IRA.
8. McDonagh and Boland, a firm of accountants whose names suggest a connection with leading figures in the national movement.
9. The family of Boss Croker of Tammany Hall fame who had a residence in South County Dublin.

Letter 183

Kitty, to Mícheál, 31 May 1922.

My own darling Mícheál,

When I got your letter to-day I was very worried to think that you never had a word from me. It seemed so hard-hearted, but each day I said to myself that he'll be back before this letter gets to London. All my letters are at the Gresham for you. I wrote you a long letter yesterday giving you all my news, and I nearly missed the post before finishing it in the long run.

I am very sorry that you are having such trouble in London. Don't know how you don't get exasperated and fed up.

I am longing to see you on Saturday. So, lovie, you will be sure to come if you can, and we will spend a day at the lake. It must have been beastly hot in London as it's the limit here. I am in great form, T.G., and never felt better.

So, isn't that cheery? I don't do much since I came home! I feel very happy. If only you could have a rest and less worry I'd be delighted. It must be wonderful at Greystones just now. I had no weather like that while I was there. It would be lovely if you could stay on there — only it is so far from your work. I mean it's so late when you get finished — but even those late nights did you some good, because if you were living in town you'd meet the boys, and they would have you up half the night. I couldn't imagine I was nearly a month there. It only seemed like a week, I mean the night part of it, I mean the length of time *we* spent together. Did you feel that way too?

We are all very sorry here for poor Joe McGuinness, R.I.P.[1] He was a very genuine sort of man, and I liked him very much and got on well always with him. I thought he looked ill when we met him that evening, but little did I think that would be my last time to see him.

Do you remember the boy Collings I introduced you to one night at the Grand?[2] I enclose his letter. His father lives at Belturbet, and this boy and his sister are decent to Chrys, so perhaps you would tell me what I should do about his father. I got this letter to-day. Chrys wrote to George about it.

Will say good bye now, darling (Am I getting very affectionate?) Bye bye my very best love, my own Mícheál, with heaps of kisses.

Yours,
Kit.

1. Joe McGuinness, the deputy for Longford who had supported the Treaty.
2. We have failed to identify this boy.

Letter 184

Kitty, to Mícheál, 1 June 1922.

My own dear Mícheál,

If I don't deserve any credit, I am certainly not getting it for sitting patiently waiting for you to return from London. Each day I think to myself he may be back from

London before this letter arrives, and in yours to-day you say
that I may not be thinking of you. Well I'll try and be
patient, as it's the only thing to do! When I came back first
I was so lonely for you, and then also I so missed Greystones
that I would just love to have packed up and gone off for
over a week. Then I thought of London, but the shock of
my unexpected arrival might upset you, otherwise I'd fly
to you. Now don't be vexed, because I'd have loved this.

You will get all my letters together. Of course I'd prefer
if you got them each day separately, but from here it takes
two days to get to London — don't you remember last
year? — whereas yours take only one day. Come as early as
you can on Saturday. Picture me forbidding you to come.
Ah, Ducky, you don't mean it.

There will be a small parcel at the Gresham for me on
Saturday. Will you take it please to me? You can then be
imagining that it's off to Greystones you are going, and tell
the driver it's Broadstone for Granard so that you come
here instead. You came early one Saturday and you brought
me a few parcels. Do you remember?

Wish I was by an icy sea tonight, it is so hot. It must be the
devil in London.

Heaps and heaps and heaps of love and a big kiss. Don't
you miss 'How can I live without you — how *can* I let you
go?' You heard nothing in London like it, never fear, and,
if you did, you wouldn't recognise it.[1]

Bye bye old sport,

Your own little pal,
Kit.

1. 'How can I live without you — how can I let you go?' Words from a
   popular romantic song to which Kitty appears to have introduced
   Mícheál.

Letter 185

Kitty, to Mícheál, Friday, received Saturday 3 June 1922.

My very dear Mícheál,

By this time I am sure you will have got all my letters, four
I think. I like your week-end in London! Was surprised today

when I got your letter as I thought you had left yesterday morning. The heat must have been awful there and I don't blame you for being fed up, and you must have had lots of worry and trouble. Were you thinking of Greystones all the time, and the lovely coolness there, and wishing you were there. I am wishing in this lovely weather that I was there now instead of May, but you know I enjoyed May too.

Larry and Paul went to Joe McGuinness's funeral R.I.P. Seán McKeown is getting married on the 20th, the day after the election I believe. Some time ago there was a rumour of it, but I didn't think it would be so soon. I believe Eoin O'Duffy will be best man for Seán. I suppose G[earóid] will be down with you tomorrow. It is not quite so hot here to-day as it was for some days past.

I feel somehow that this is a very uninteresting letter, but I'll keep all the news till I see you.

Don't forget my little parcel at the Gresham, but I should not say this as you never forget anything. I am, needless to tell you, looking forward to seeing you and I wish you were coming to stay a month with me but, Ducky, I'll try to be satisfied with the two days. So don't worry that I'll make a fuss. I promised in Greystones that we would have no more rows, so I'll try to stick to it. They were more or less my fault, but if I didn't care we'd never have a row. You are not supposed to read this last line, but you couldn't resist it.

Good bye for one day, my lovie, my sweetheart and everything.

Best love from
Kit.

Don't forget the London papers, if you have them.

Letter 186

Kitty, to Mícheál, Monday, received Wednesday, 7 June 1922.

My own dear Mícheál,

I am afraid this will have to be a very short note as it's getting near posting time.

I hope you got back to town safely and that you got to bed fairly early.

I am very lonely for you, and am sorry for having such a row and upsetting our last few hours together. Especially as I didn't want a row. If you read Saturday's letter you can see this. I try to feel every time I am with you that each time might be my last time with you and try to make it as happy as possible. However, perhaps the next time I ask you to that bed I'll be like I was the night before,[1] 'Nothing will vex me'. Some sweeping statement!

I hope your cold is better. I have got it in my head now. When I suggested that little rest yesterday, it was because of your cold and you looked tired. But I know you can resist sleep, so I made up my mind in a second to ask you out. And then I would have liked it too. Better luck next time, sweetheart. I'll write a long letter later.

I hope you are as happy as I want to be? Write a long letter.

With my fondest love,

Your own,
Kit.

I didn't go to the races. You know one of the reasons.

Love,
Kit.

Hugs and kisses which no one will ever get but ——.

K.K.

1. Read this with Letter 187. Whenever she found Mícheál, on coming to Granard, in an exhausted condition, she tried to get him to lie down for a few hours.

Letter 187

Kitty, to Mícheál, Tuesday, received Wednesday, 7 June 1922.

My own dear Mícheál,

The disappointment was all the greater this morning when I got no letter because I was anxious to know if you got back safely, and if your cold had gone. Then I wondered if the row on Sunday evening had anything to do with no letter. Thank the Lord it hadn't, because I would have been disappointed in you, and it would make a bad impression on me.

Needless for me to say how sorry I am that you couldn't get to Cork. I don't want to be rubbing it in, but your cold was nearly gone when you came in from tennis. It was the little lie down and the little sleep on the lounge that gave it to you again. You were, I'm sure, in a draught. I was going to cover you but was afraid you might wake up and think that I wanted you. I did want you but I would not awaken you. Would I? But you must be more careful for my sake, even apart from yourself. I was in bed to-day, with a cold in my head, mostly. It's nearly gone now.

We had a delightful day at Omard yesterday. Went there at 7 o'c, Paul, Vi, Maud and I, to explain away my absence on Sunday. We played tennis and danced afterwards. At least 'Bachelor gay'[1] and myself performed. There were a few men there, but don't think that I even bothered looking at them, and you misunderstand about Harry. I was only 'trying' to tease you. Don't be vexed with me.

I'd love to be near you to-day, sweetheart, and, in the words of Harry, to make 'sacred and profane love' to you. It is lovely the way I can hide my love from you, as I don't think you know. But if you did, it wouldn't make any difference I think. Sure it wouldn't, lovie? I mean you would think more of me, wouldn't you? Answer this question 'faithfully', because you never answer my important questions. Forgot on Sunday to ask you about Fred Collings. What will I say to him? I haven't written yet.

G[earóid] is coming by motor to-morrow night to take Mops to town on Thursday morning for shopping. So I am going too, and dear, I know you are ever so busy and we will shop and, if you have time at night, then I will want you. We are only staying two days. I am getting a new white suit; I hope you will like it.

Now, my own Mícheál, good bye. Will let you know when we get to town on Thursday.

With all my love to you. Ever your own little pet,

Kit.

1. Probably Paul.

Letter 188

Kitty, to Mícheál, received 8 June 1922.

My dear Mícheál,

After a storm comes a calm. The boat had only left
Dunleary (can't spell it)[1] when you wrote a letter to me.
While you were in London every day, amid the excitement
and worry, you wrote. Then came that 'you will have to see
me Saturday evening'. This you said every day. I began to
think to myself, I wonder what will happen after he's seen
me on Satuday night? It was very gushing. Now I wouldn't
mind if you had fallen in with my suggestions made ages
ago that you write and I write once a week. Then I wouldn't
expect. But not at all. *You* wouldn't have this.

It wouldn't have hurt you yesterday to write me two
lines. You left here Sunday evening. Monday and Tuesday
and Wednesday and no word of you, but one wire. Mícheál,
I know you are awfully busy, but I can see through it all the
same. You saw me and you were quite satisfied and I hadn't
run away with anyone! It is the first time you *ever* did this,
but then you were fearfully busy. You were never so busy
before. Good luck to you. Hope you are better; some day
I'll get my own back.

Yours, Kit.

P.S. Have just got a wire from you. I withdraw part of what
I said, but there is still some truth in it. As before you wrote
and you lying up, not that I expected you'd write and you
ill, but you did it nevertheless, but you don't do those sort
of silly things now! My love till I see you.   K.K.

1. Dun Laoghaire had not yet officially replaced Kingstown as the
   name of the seaside town six miles on the south side of Dublin.
   Kitty was trying to spell the word as she would have heard it pro-
   nounced.

Letter 189

Kitty, to Mícheál, 12 June 1922.

My very dear Mícheál,

I hope you got back in good form and in good time. We

had a lovely run home. We went to bed almost immediately.
We both felt tired.

I hope your cold has gone so that you can enjoy your tour
in Cork. When are you going? Please remember me to Seán[1]
and Mrs Powell[2] if you see her.

I needn't apologise now for all the little rows, as I did so
last night in Mullingar before you left. Isn't that right? I am
feeling happy now because I know you forgive me and don't
misunderstand my peculiarities. I told you about them often
before, but I think it is only a passing thing, and not really
my real self. But the sad part of it is that I make you suffer
as well as myself, and, of course, I'm sorry always afterwards.
I know it's not exactly fair to you because I must say you do
your best, and would want to be with me more if you could.
It is not my nature to be so narrow and mean, and nobody
could be more disgusted than I with myself sometimes.

I seek consolation sometimes in the fact that I've been
ill and I don't suppose I told you all the doctor said. He
didn't want to tell me when I went first, but I must be six
years ill, he says now, and that I had been nervous and highly
strung and easily irritated, that it will pass away very soon
if I have lots of rest and no worry. He wouldn't hear of my
leaving Greystones, as I was getting perfect. He said I had got
such frights and worry for a young person with my
temperament that quietness was the best thing for me at
present. So it is probably the reaction when I am with
you. I get so excited when I see you, because you are the
only one I love with all my heart, and I take too much out
of myself at first and then get burnt up! And then perhaps
you see the tears, and *you* know that I love to shed a few
just for you — for no reason at all — but just for you. I mean
they are reserved for you. Very pleasant for you, I must
admit! Poor Ducky, if only you knew how much I'd love to
give you to make you happy, and to help you in every way
in all your worries and everything, and to be your friend,
partner, sweetheart, and everything in a woman that you
want. And if only I was strong I think I could be nearly
everything to you.

Hope you slept all right and that I was fairly near so
that you could imagine _____.

Hope to see you soon whenever you can come. And now bye bye my own Mícheál. Your little pet sends you all the love you want, with heaps of kisses and hugs.

Your own
Kit.

1. Collins's brother Seán, John or Johnnie.
2. His sister Mary.

Letter 190

Kitty, to Mícheál, 13 June 1922.

My own dear Mícheál,

I was glad to get your letter this morning but sorry that you had to trot off to London again. I knew from to-day's paper that you had gone for certain. You won't get my letter of yesterday until you return again and I'm sorry, as I think it was a fairly nice one.

I hope your cold has gone completely. You don't say.

Yes, the month was a short one. I only like the months to be short with you. Concerning a letter from you, I got your letter and your wire. I liked them.

We didn't play tennis last week as it came wet, so we had music in Paul's instead. There is a race meeting in Longford to-morrow and we all expect to go. Hope I'll have more luck than at the [Phoenix] Park, but that was because you were there.

Poor Darrell Figgis[1] lost his nice red beard. When I read about it I could imagine you laughing and enjoying it very much. But it was a mean thing for some of Harry's cronies to do, wasn't it? Funny, this ages I've been expecting that something might happen to Figgis (from reading the papers). He was lucky it was only his beard.

I enclose a little cutting from the *Daily Mirror*. I was going to send you *The Roscommon Herald* — nothing concerning you and I but it was interesting this week. Then I thought you wouldn't have time to read it.

Paul McGovern is coming here to-night on his way back from town where he was for a day. He goes to Cavan tomorrow and back to Enniskillen. Helen is in good form I believe.

I hope you get on well in Cork, and that the trip will do you good. It will be a bit of a change for you. I hope you will have some sleep tho'.

I am writing to your sister the nun at last! I'll tell her that I've been ill and not allowed to write letters, which is quite true. I was wondering what I could do for you that you would like me to do, so I decided on this. Is that all right?

I am feeling in great form to-day T.G. I went to bed and slept well and I'm going to Mass for you and I won't forget the candle either.

I may have left a gap between two words in yesterday's letter. If so the word is 'apologise'.

I am still full of sorrow for not being nicer in town. I don't really know what happened to me unless it was nerves. I wish you were here now. You would see a difference. It is extraordinary how everything looks through different glasses when one is well and happy. When you have time again I want you to get me a cheap edition of *The Little White Bird*[2] 2/- as I want to send it to Mrs Doyle;[3] the one she gave me is a 'bit' soiled.

Now bye bye, sweetheart, with my fondest love and the best of good luck.

Lovingly,
Kit.

1. Darrell Figgis (1882-1925), a colourful character who, at different times, was honorary secretary of Sinn Féin, editor of *The Republic*, secretary to a Dáil Committee of Inquiry into the Resources and Industries of Ireland, and chairman of the 1922 Constitution Committee. He represented Co. Dublin in the Dáil.
2. *The Little White Bird*, a novel by J. M. Barrie whom Mícheál had met in London.
3. Mrs Leigh-Doyle — See note to Letter No. 63.

Letter 191

Kitty, to Mícheál, Thursday, received 20 June 1922.

My own dear Mícheál,

Thanks for your letter received to-day. I hope you got my second letter before leaving for Cork.

When in Longford yesterday evening I 'phoned the Office to see if you had gone to Cork.

We had a great day's racing. I backed four winners. Some change for me.

I hope you get this all right. I like the way you give me your address. If I wished I could pretend I didn't know where I'd be *sure* to find you, and so not write.

Will you be back for Seán's wedding? I got no invitation from Miss Cooney and, of course, I wouldn't go on the invitation that you got, if you got any at all for me? However, I don't really want to go, but would *love* you to go and enjoy it. You can make any excuse for me, as when she didn't write I wouldn't go and I never met Seán since, and I'd only be asked because of you, and that's that!

I hope you have a good time in Cork. You got a great reception anyway by the papers. You must have had an awful rush in London. I hope your cold has gone?

Mrs McLaverty was at races yesterday. No man hanging on to her for a change. Of course she enquired for you. 'She went to London with Mr Griffith'. Poor Griffith was a bit dull, I'm sure. I think she said she didn't meet you. What a pity *she* wasn't *the* Lady and not Lady L. in the car,[1] just what she would like. Very sad. It would be worth even the Doctor divorcing her to cause a sensation in London — just her style I imagine. I don't think I'd ever marry if I had to be a Mrs McL.

I am feeling in great form T.G. and must see about going away later.

Two American priests have just called to see me — on your account, of course.

Do excuse hurried note as I have to rush to get post.

Good bye, dearest. My fondest love.

Yours,

Kit.

Good luck. Sorry I haven't the little black cat to send you. Not even a velvet one.

---

1. See Letter 178. The Laverys had been photographed driving Collins to Downing Street. Some newspapers 'played up' the picture of Collins with 'his sweetheart'. The lady with Sir John was, however, Sir John's wife Hazel.

Letter 192

Kitty, to Mícheál, Friday, received 23 June 1922.

My own dear Mícheál,

Just a line in awful haste. Hope you are A.1. I was coming
from the pictures last night about 11 o'c and I saw a big
car same as yours in the dark at our door. I knew it couldn't
be you, so I asked the driver who he had and he said Mr
Boland is inside. And there was Harry and a Mr O'Donovan
T.D. from Kerry.[1] O'Donovan left later for Dublin, but
Harry stayed and is here to-day. He got a very cold reception
and no invitation to stay. I didn't see him only once to-day,
but I just 'killed' him. O'Donovan isn't bad. We gave him a
bit about Harry too. I felt like saying to H. — well you knew
'he' wouldn't be here this time anyway.

The voting is going on all right here. Great excitement
but no rows.

Excuse this note. Will write later. Rushing for post.

My fondest love and everything till Tuesday or when?

Always,
Your loving
Kit.

I am sure you are busy to-day. H. is 'killing' in to-day's paper
on the Constitution.

1. She appears to have got the name wrong. The visitor with Harry
   was Thomas O'Donoghue, one of the deputies for Kerry and West
   Limerick.

Letter 193

Kitty, to Mícheál, Friday, received 26 June 1922.

My own darling Mícheál,

I was delighted to get your little note to-day. Also delighted
with results from Cork. Everybody seems charmed too.

G[earóid] came down last night and went back on the 12
from Mullingar to-day. I left Maud and himself alone and
went up to bed to Larry's room, and I was wishing that you
were still here. I went to bed thinking of you and planning

all sorts, a lovely house (not an elaborate one) but an artistic, bright and comfortable one, and it would be *'Ours'*. You know one of those lovely moods, when you see everything beautiful and artistic. I could picture so many things. Then I went to sleep and awoke again this morning continuing my dream. We will be ever so happy and you will see how I'll try to make our home, be it small or large, a happy one for you.

The queerest things come into my head sometimes. I thought again this morning, later on, that you were in my bed, that this Kitty was no more, but that in my place was a little kid (ours), that it was the image of me, and that you had your arm around it, loving it because it reminded you of me. Then I tried to picture you were no more. That a little boy, the image of you, was beside me. How I would love it and mind it if it was like you, and so on. It must have been our conversation about your little Cork child that put all this into my head.

Please excuse pencil. I hope you are well and cold gone. Shall write a long one later. Good bye. My fond love to you.

Your own
Kit.

Letter 194

Mícheál, Cork, to Kitty, 24 June 1922, telegram.

Have finished with the counting at last. Wound up at about seven o'clock this morning. Am returning Dublin to-day. Will write or wire you when I get back. How are you?

M.

Letter 195

Mícheál, Dublin, to Kitty, 24 June 1922 (night), telegram

Thanks for letter. I have returned safely and will write to you to-morrow. M.

Letter 196

Kitty, to Mícheál, Saturday [24 June 1922]

My very dear Mícheál,

    I was expecting a letter to-day but I was delighted to get even a wire.

    The results were very good in Cork. I am sure you are very pleased.

    By this time I suppose you are back in Dublin and have got my letters. I hope you will like them. I didn't bother writing to Cork, as I don't like the idea of my letters floating about in the post maybe. Excuse this letter but I have a bad headache which I must have got while sewing. I was experimenting on a poor camisole for the past half-hour, and it does not look too bad at all, 'tho not worth a headache.

    How is poor old lovie? Very tired I'm sure. Think of it, you won't get this till Monday. I wish you were to be here to-morrow, but you will be very busy now, and I suppose I can't lament, now that I saw you once in a week, even tho' it was very short at the end.

    Paul, Mops and I went into the country yesterday evening, and had tea in a little cottage. It was delightful. I was wishing you were there. We walked part of the way and drove the rest. We enjoyed it well. The weather here is rainy and cold all the time. How is your cold? When am I going up to nurse you?

    I send you one big hug and a kiss and all my love, and please excuse this uninteresting letter.

Your own,
Kitty.

P.S. I forgot to show you the enclosed cutting from an American paper while you were here, but everything goes out of my head when you are here. Write a long long long letter soon. The kind you usually write, Ducky.

Love again
from
K.

Letter 197

My own darling Mícheál,

If you could see me now going around in flat low-heeled shoes, you would know I was trying to please you.

I hope you got back safely and that you did find the cushion and ring useful. Also I hope that you were able to sleep in spite of the jolting of the car on bad roads. Did you forget and sit on the bottle and break it, or did you need it? I hope you had it.

I am very lonely after you, but happy that we made it up. It seems almost a tragedy that we should have such frightful misunderstandings. I am my own worst enemy in this, and come out very badly when all is said and done. I do hope I'll be different, but I'm going to try for your happiness as well as my own, for I do realise how unhappy I make things for you too. It is all so stupid also, especially when I have such a tremendous corner for you (I mean the whole thing, of course, but it won't be well to know this!).

Well, lovie, I *was* anxious to go [away] with you last night, but I also had another feeling, a desperate [feeling]. If I had gone with you, it might have been for good. (I can't exactly describe it, but perhaps you understand.) I'd have stayed with you, I'd have wanted to. Last night was a real wedding night for you and me. Didn't you feel that way too, but couldn't put it into words? I *wanted* to run away with you. That must be the feeling with people who do run away like that. We had it last night. That was our night.

Glad to-day, for *both you and me*, that I did not go. Isn't this right? *Tell* me. Do — am I not right? Heaps of kisses that you should have got yesterday, and heaps and heaps of hugs and love and love and hugs and kisses.

> Your own little pet,
> Kit.

What about that little cough? I hope it will go soon. I feel I want to write you about all my little plans and the love that I've got for you.

> K.

Letter 198

Mícheál, Dublin, to Kitty, 26 June 1922.

My own dearest Kitty,

I got both your letters this morning; the earlier one was here when I came back on Saturday evening. They were all very nice and I was delighted with them. Is there any chance of you coming to town during the week? I stayed at Greystones on Saturday night — the first real sleep I had for a week. Talk of being tired — and am still very tired. It's awful. Am going to Greystones again tonight, so there's a little hope for another sleep. Do come up please please.

The idea of you in low heels — I was only half serious you know.

That's an extraordinary idea of yours. On Friday morning I had little Brenda[1] in the bed with me and I was thinking of her being ours. Isn't that queer?

Must finish this — the usual thing. Everyone waiting, God help me — take this note for what it ought to be — about 12 pages long. God be with you, Kitty dear.

> Fondest love,
> Your
> Mícheál.

1. Not identified.

Letter 199

Kitty to Mícheál, Monday [possibly 3 July 1922].

My own dear Mícheál,

Wish I had the art of writing a letter with very little in it and yet a lot.

Many thanks for your long letter received to-day. I had been looking forward to it for ages. I got a real feeling of sadness, and felt like crying while reading it.

Now just at this moment I perhaps see things in a different light but *just then* I said, 'Why is he afraid to write his love all through the letter as I do, and then end up with just an "M"?' The first and best goes to Ireland, I am only a good second, at least at the present time. Almost a year ago you would have written a more affectionate letter under the circumstances. That would only take a few seconds and would have pleased me. But, indeed, just as I said before, *now* I see it in a different light, and your letter to-day was very nice, and it was good of you to write at all, and you so worried and upset. Still, darling, a sentence would have satisfied me, if I was sure you really missed *me*, and had not somebody else. Knowing a little about you that, if you really wanted me badly, you would wire or write as you often did to have me near you and even if I did not go, I'd have loved to *feel* you did really want me. Now, don't please think I am referring to the letter to-day saying they are imprinted on my mind like nothing else.

I'll be *great* with you, and have no rows, please God. Oh! how I hate them and I'll be counting the days until you come to see me. It's years and years since we were first great friends.

Love again,
Yours as ever,
Kit.

Letter 200

Mícheál, Dublin, to Kitty, 2 July 1922, telegram.

Am still all right. Have not heard from you for several days. Probably your letters are in the hands of the others at the Gresham. We will redeem them yet. God be with you.

Love, M.

Letter 201

Mícheál, Dublin, to Kitty, 2 July 1922, telegram.

Received all your letters to-day on my return. Shall see you on Saturday evening same time.

Love, M.

Letter 202

Kitty, to Mícheál, fragment of a letter, early July 1922.

. . . that O'Connell St is an awful sight. I realise and appreciate that, and would hate to see it, but then that is not you.

There we differ. It isn't O'Connell St I want, it's you. I'd
hate to go, and have no intention of going, and your remark
was quite justified and wise, as it must be depressing and I'd
hate and do not want to go, and it's all away from that point.
It's the spirit of the thing. If I wasn't such a good judge
and know you better than you think. However, dearest,
it's all over now, and I hope you can come soon, and please
forgive me if I am unreasonable. But that's me. You will
have to bear that, until I get sense (just as I feel I bear
some things too!).

You did not say how you are but that's a detail! and I
would not like to hear. Yet your letter *was* really lovely,
and I mean this. But did you ever get a lovely letter and were
not satisfied; but I'm not so bad now as when I first got it.

Now don't think too hard of me this time — as I am half
sorry for saying so much — but if you saw me today with
big tears of disappointment you'd forgive.

Your own loving pet,

Kit ('K').

Do you still want a big hug and a kiss because I send them;
and you sent me not one kiss.

Letter 203

Mícheál, Dublin, to Kitty, circa 5 July 1922.

Kitty dear,

This is a really unpleasant letter, but I cannot pretend to
be in good humour when I am not. You know me better
than I think? And who's the somebody else? And O'Connell
St is broken down and I'm sorry that the poor old
Gresham is gone and destroyed. But it is gone, and I suppose
I can't restore it or can I or what? And what must I do?

And now I'm called. So goodnight and love and everything.
And if I'm in places where I can't even wire to you or where
you don't hear at all of me or from me, I'll think of you and
it will be all the harder because you won't know and harder
still because you'll be wondering that you don't hear and all
sorts of things. What I mean is, you'll say it's my fault. And
if it's not, there'll be no one to say it's not. And that's that.
And, fondest love, no matter what.

Mícheál.

Letter 204

Mícheál, Dublin, to Kitty, 5 July 1922, telegram.

Things have got quieter. Here at least they are quieter this morning. Hope ordinary conditions will be restored in a few days. How are you and everything? Too soon yet to talk about visiting or writing. All here doing well so far. Fondest love to you.

M.

Letter 205

Kitty, to Mícheál, 6 July 1922, telegram.

Delighted to hear from you and hope to see you soon. All here well and very quiet. Best love from,

Kitty.

Letter 206

Mícheál, Dublin, to Kitty, 7 July 1922, telegram.

Your letter of Wednesday received to-day. Ever so many thanks. You'll have to find another address now the Gresham is gone. Use 44 Mountjoy Street. Things are quiet enough to-day.

[no name]

Letter 207

Kitty, to Mícheál, Wednesday, received 7 July 1922.

My own darling Mícheál,

I hope you are all right. All sorts of alarming rumours came in here to-day, that Dublin was nearly as bad as Easter Week. So you can picture me. A few more grey hairs for sure, to add to the number.

I was delighted to get your little note. I know you are killed with work. You should go to Greystones at night — not *too* late — to get some sleep. I forgot to ask you, after you mentioned Greystones before, what room you had, and if you missed me, and were very lonely because I was not there? I liked it and wish I was there now and you coming out in the evening. It was great.

You didn't answer the simplest little question I asked you in my letter of Thursday last. You must have forgotten.

How did you like yesterday's letter? *I* have to do all the telling. I mean, even if you felt it, you wouldn't write 'that life was sad without me'! or anything half so nice. However, I don't mind that, and will forgive you. I meant yesterday's letter all right, and even to-day, when I think of you perhaps in the midst of a fight, I think that I should be near you, beside you. Because if you were going to die, I'd like to go with you. Now I am not sentimental, though I suppose you think I am. I do wish that I was with you now. I am always thinking of you, every day more and more, so you ought to be happy.

I suppose you can't come this week. I might be able to go next, but I wouldn't like to go this week and leave Mops. Larry went to town to-day via Nobber, so I suppose he's not there yet.

Good bye, lovie. With heaps of hugs, kisses, and best love from your own

Kitty.

This is a little change from the last few letters. I told you a lot of things in them, so now I just send you all my love, again. Write to me *if* you can a newsy letter about yourself, and say if you are lonely for me. And good bye and good luck.

K.

Letter 208

Kitty to Mícheál, Thursday, received 8 July 1922.

My very dear Mícheál,

I got a letter from you to-day which was written on 28 June. I had it read before I saw the date and was wondering! There can be only one letter of mine which you may not have got, as there is no post here since Wednesday last. There is no necessity for me to say how glad I was to get word from you on Sunday. I knew if you could have wired sooner you would. I got it from Oldcastle about 11 o'c here; hope you got mine all right. I was going out to Mass or I'd have sent a longer message and, as it was, I was almost late for Mass.

Last week was the longest one I ever spent, but I couldn't have believed that I'd survive so well. Of course I was longing *all the time* to be with you, and at first I was terrified that you would take all kinds of risks. And how I wished to be near you (and I felt that I *should* have been) so that I could put my arms tightly around your neck, and that nothing could happen you. And, of course, I was wishing we were married, because then I would be surely near you, and happy.

I'd have chanced getting to Dublin, but then I thought you mightn't like this, and I said to myself I'd please you in this, at least I'd do what I thought you would like me to do, and so I tried to be patient. It was very hard. Would you *have loved* to have had me, or would I be in the way? Because you know I wouldn't be a bit afraid when I'd be beside you. And if you were killed, I'd be dying with you, and that would be great, and far better than if I were left alone behind. I'd be very much alone if you were gone. Nothing could change that, and all last week and this I've realised it, and that's what makes it so hard. However, God is good and I'm putting all my trust in Him. Part of the time I couldn't pray, I felt so unhappy. No matter how bad I was, I could get no word from you. I was going to try 'phoning from Longford or some place, but I waited on and then didn't go to Longford at all. It seems very hard-hearted, but what could I do? I am not a bit certain that this letter will reach you. So I'll not say much more.

The papers came to-day. It is a scandal to think of all those lovely buildings gone, including the poor Gresham. Nearly every day we saw a paper, but they didn't console *me* much. I was charmed with your wire yesterday, but I think I set even more value on Sunday's one, because it was the first from you.

I hope I'll see you very soon and give you all the news. No excitement here at all.

Have you slept much? Those are the sort of things that are troubling me *most* of all.

It is absurd all the worry and work you have had on your shoulders, but God is good.

Good bye sweetheart. All my love from

Your devoted, Kit.

191

Letter 209

Kitty, to Mícheál, Saturday [8 July 1922].

My very dear Mícheál,

I was delighted to get your wire yesterday and to know you are well. I wrote to you on Thursday to 44. I am surprised you didn't get it yesterday as the posts are going all right here now for the past few days. It was no use writing sooner than Thursday as the post didn't go out. I am looking forward to a letter from you. So I hope you will be able to write a line to-day sometime and I may get it on Monday.

You must feel very tired and fed up, but glad that there is such victory. Poor Cathal Brugha, R.I.P. A pitiable ending for a fruitless gain.[1]

I am all alone to-day. Mops went up to E[2] just for the week end and I may go next. Chrys and Tom are there, also Vi, all having a good time I'm sure! I suppose you are staying at 44 all the time. What will you do at the week end? Work, I suppose. I enclose an *Independent* photograph. Very like Harry going off with the visitors.

Did Mrs McLaverty visit you, or *vice a versa*? [*sic*] Don't say you had no ladies to look after you, during the trouble? They seem to have been active enough.

We played tennis whenever we had a fine day. Not very often. It rains here indefinitely.

Excuse short note, but it's post time. Good bye. Best love and good luck to you from Kit.

How is George & Co.?

1. Brugha, formerly Chief of Staff of the IRA and Minister for Defence in Dáil Éireann, having strenuously opposed the Treaty, joined the Irregular forces in the Civil War and was killed on 5 July 1922 as he came, firing, out of Granville Hotel in O'Connell St, Dublin.   2. Enniskillen.

Letter 210

Kitty, to Mícheál, Tuesday [11 July 1922], a pencilled note.

My own dear Mícheál,

Just a little note. I hope you are well? Please excuse the

pencil writing. Mops is back. Paul Cusack was in town during
the fighting. It was rumoured he was fighting. Just a yarn.

I am looking forward to seeing you soon. I had no letter
to-day but I hope to get one tomorrow, and that you won't
be too cross for yesterday's letter. I was very sorry
afterwards, but I thought it better to tell you when I felt
it at the time. Please, do please, forgive me as I wish to-day
I hadn't felt like I did. I love you much, as ever, and am
longing to be with you again, but I quite understand the
extraordinary way you are placed and so busy and everything,
and sympathise with you and only wish I was of real use to
you, but I knew you would say now that nice letters would
be the best, but, sure, wasn't Thursday's of last week and
Wednesday's of the week before nice? At least the spirit
was good *all* the time, and you will never know how much
I longed to be near you during the fighting, and how much
I wished that I was beside you anywhere and not be a wee
bit nervous. You may not believe that I wouldn't be nervous
but it is true I think, and I send you a big big kiss and hugs,
and I send myself in spirit to you. So bye bye.

> Love from your own
> Kit.

Letter 211

Mícheál, Dublin, to Kitty, 12 July 1922, telegram.

Haven't heard from you for some days. Hope everything
well at your end. Communications bad generally. Did
you get my letter? Love.

> M.

Letter 212

Kitty, to Mícheál, 12 July 1922, telegram.

Wrote you on Thursday to 44. Many thanks for wire.
Love from

> K.

Letter 213

*Mícheál, Government Buildings, Dublin, to Kitty, 12 July
1922.*

My dearest Kitty,
Am writing this note to you very very late and will not

have it posted before midnight. Will not indeed have it written before midnight, and then I'm going off to stay some place. Am writing this at Merrion Street where I've been for the past 3 or 4 hours. When I arrived back here your letter was awaiting me and I've read it with a heavy and sad heart two or three times. Some time during the night I'll read it again — if there is light. I'll wonder why you think so harshly of me. It does seem strange, but I'm sure I am to blame although it's unconscious.

I sent you a very very hurried wire today — a boy tells me he posted it late — please do forgive me for it. There were people waiting while I wrote it. It would, I'm certain, have been much better if I hadn't written it. Not writing it would have shown how much more clearly that I was thinking of you.

May God bless you anyway,
Mícheál.

Letter 214

Mícheál, Government Buildings, Dublin, to Kitty, 13 July 1922.

Kitty dearest,

I have had to come in here this morning — it's only 8 o'clock — and your letter is lying here not yet posted.[1] You'll read this note before the other one — in fact don't read the other one at all, if you like. I know it's nasty, but your letter was a bit *upsetting* and I was absolutely tired and worn out after a terrible day. So there you are. And I'm longing to see you and everything and all my love and, wherever I may be for the next week, I'll do my very best to wire and write. And God be with you, my own Kitty.

'M'.

1. He means the letter he had written to her around midnight on 12 July (Letter 213).

Letter 215

Mícheál, Dublin, to Kitty, 14 July 1922.

My own dearest Kitty,

Your letter which got to me late last night was very

welcome. I don't know what I'd have done if it had been
like that of the day before. I wonder what you thought
of mine — did you read the nasty one? Although there is
little doubt. However I do hope I shall see you within
the next four or five days but, of course, one never knows.
At any rate I'll do my best.

Dublin is much quieter again, but for the past few days
I've seen little of it, at least little of the broken up portion.

Tell me, how are you? One thing — don't worry about me.
I have every faith in things coming right no matter how
difficult and dark the outlook at the moment. Then we shall
be happier, and I hope all the happier because of what we've
been through.

With all my love,

Mícheál.

Letter 216

Kitty, to Mícheál, Thursday, received 15 July 1922.

My own darling Mícheál,

I was very disappointed yesterday when I got your wire
to think that you didn't get any of my letters. I wrote a long
letter on Thursday last which I think you got. You said so
in Saturday morning's wire. I wrote on Saturday, Monday
and Tuesday. Perhaps by now they have turned up. I got one
letter from you altogether. Of course I was always expecting
one, but I know you can't write. How are you? You must be
killed with work. I hope you are not vexed with me for
Monday's letter.

I went to bed last night about 9 o'c and, of course, I
couldn't sleep, so I was talking to you and my heart ached
with longing to have you with me. I was 'madly, passionately,
in love with you', to use your own words, and I understand
those feelings now, and I feel that I'm blushing now because
I tell you. But sure you know and we both know and
remember Greystones and all the other wonderful times.

Then I went through all the stages of the future, until
I came to the kind of matter-of-fact stage when we are so
used to each other that it would be uncomfortable, cold and

something gone wrong, if one or other were not there. We mightn't admit it, but it would be a natural sort of feeling. We would wake up in the middle of the night, and not be able to sleep peacefully, because there was that something, something not exactly explainable. Now, sure, I wasn't building castles in the air with those dreams. Is not that what will happen? And I forgot to tell you that I decided last night that it was that matter-of-fact stage I liked best, I think.

I think I am really continuing last night's little romance to-day. Of course, I couldn't tell you here all the nice things I said last night to you, all the love and everything I gave you, or will give you, and I found myself promising you faithfully that I'd never have a real row, nor fall out with you at all, no matter what you did, 'if', first, you are sympathetic to me (now don't laugh, because I'm real serious), if you are not too rough, and don't hurt me when we are just playing, just fooling, and a few other little ifs.

I hope to see you soon. It's three weeks yesterday. A very very long time, but God is good.

I enclose the nun's letter. I got a letter — which I must show you when you come — from Australia, from a man who wants to know when is my wedding, as the ladies there want to send me a presentation, and say lovely things about you. I got it on Monday last.

I'll say bye bye now, I hope you will like this letter. I mean it to be very nice, but can't write as nicely as I felt last night. It was great. You were just beside me. I had a sleeveless arm around your neck. It was so long that it went around your neck twice.

All my love.

Your own,
Kit.

Letter 217

Kitty, to Mícheál, Saturday [15 July 1922].

My own darling Mícheál,

Picture my surprise this morning when I got your wire saying that my letters were wrongly addressed tho' I had a suspicion of this myself, as one day I discovered my mistake in time! It was very stupid of me. I could have kicked myself to-day. So now I address the envelope first so as to make sure! We used to stay in Mountjoy Square so that must be why I do it.

I am A.1., thank God, altho' I'm writing in bed, but I'm only lying down resting. I hope you are well. I was just delighted to get your letter to-day, and I'm longing to see you. Hope you got my Thursday letter by this, as it tells you how much I am longing.

You are C. in Chief now. What does this mean? More trouble I suppose. Will it ever end? But God is good.

I wish that we were already married, and that the very next time we'd meet was on our honeymoon — would you like it also? — because I feel I'll never let you go the next time without me, and then what would you do? But maybe I will let you go. I'll say this anyway in case it would frighten you. You mightn't come at all!

Excuse writing from bed. Do you sleep at all? I think of you every night. Indeed you are *never* forgotten by me. I wish you knew.

All my love to you.

Your own little pet,
Kit.

Larry is back from town, also Vi and Paul. I didn't see Paul yet. I was nearly sending you a bit of my hair. I mean one hair, not a silver one tho'. How lonely I'll be tomorrow, and how I'll be wishing you were here.

Do excuse writing. It's the devil in bed, and bad any time.

Letter 218

Kitty, to Mícheál, Friday, received 15 July 1922.

My own darling Mícheál,

There was a great post to-day. I was washing my hair — only half-expecting a letter — so as not to be too disappointed, when two letters came from you. It made up for the disappointment yesterday. When I read them, if you had only been near hand anywhere, you would have got several kisses and hugs and things, because I was in an affectionate mood and very soft towards you. When you write thus, I often feel that way, even when I am most vexed with you. There is always that anxiety, first, to be great with you but I expect you know this, and it is very easy when there are mixed feelings to start the whole thing going.

I am very sorry (I was very sorry in fact on Monday while writing to you) for upsetting you and making you unhappy, but then I was lonely for you, and I don't know how it was altogether. I felt disappointed but it lasted a short time only.

I am longing to see you. Was it ever so long before? I feel we will be greater than ever. Do you? And I think I love you more and more every day, and I am always planning to make you so happy, with a nice home and everything. This ought to cheer you up, to know that you'll have a devoted little wife and sweetheart who will do her share in everything, provided she gets all your love and attention. I hope to give you a surprise and make home everything for you, restful, peaceful, and happy. I don't care if it be ever so small, so long as I have you I don't want much else. But you will have to be satisfied too, because whatever you will want I'll want, and isn't that it?

Hope you got all my other letters. The first one I wrote I think was on Saturday last, and one on Tuesday and yesterday.

Violet, Larry, and Peggie went to town by motor on Wednesday. Paul isn't home yet. I was nearly going with them. Vi. was telling me on Monday that Mrs Brian Cusack's brother, Frank Keen — he was here when he told her — heard Cathal B., R.I.P., saying all sorts of nice things about you in Oldtown about the election time, that he only said those things to you at the Dáil to save the Republic etc., that you were one of the best men, full of energy, and that he'd like to see the man that would beat you in votes, and several other things. The Keen boy didn't tell me but [Vi] told me afterwards that it was a great surprise to them all at Oldtown.

Maud is back. She says that Paul and Helen's house is just a dream. It is gorgeous. Paul has wonderful taste. It seems a revelation to everyone. He fitted up all the beds etc. himself, invented all kinds of improvements, and is a great mechanic. He has never taken a drink since Dublin. They are ever so happy.

It is just post time, so excuse haste.

All my love.

Your own loving
Kit.

You don't say how you are. Poor old 'ducky', my own lovie. How is Mrs McL? You didn't say.

Letter 219

Mícheál, Dublin, to Kitty, 17 July 1922, telegram.

Received your two letters yesterday evening. Many many thanks. Wanted to write you yesterday but couldn't. Sending note to-day. Best love.

Mícheál.

Letter 220

Kitty, to Mícheál, Tuesday, received 20 July 1922.

My own darling Mícheál,

Delighted to get your wire yesterday and to know you were writing, but no letter came to-day. Suppose it will come to-morrow, and perhaps I won't be quite so enthusiastic. But that's the way or, as you would say, that's that. I was very disappointed because I was so sure of it, but I suppose we can't be sure of anything these days.

I was delighted you got my two letters. I wired you on Saturday as well as writing. I hope now that you have got all my letters, as you should have got one for almost every day. In Friday's night wire you said 'Arthur'[1] was back'? Did you mean anything? I forgot to ask you when writing on Saturday. And also in one of your letters — I got three altogether — you said something about the Gresham. You must have read part of my letter wrong, because I was only referring to your remark, 'that the streets looked so depressing and not to come to town'. And then I said, 'I quite understand this'. So you must have taken it up wrong, and in every letter since I meant to tell you this, and then forgot.

How are you? I am A.1., thank God. We were in Omard[2] on Saturday, and I spent most of the time in the garden pulling and eating strawberries, and then cream and strawberries when I was tired pulling them. They were asking for and praying for you.

I believe poor Callaghan's[3] funeral was great, R.I.P. Seán McKeon was there in great form, I hear. Things are very quiet here, thank God.

Mops was thinking of going up for a day and a night. G[earóid] asked her, as he can't come down, to go to Greystones and he could get off for a night, but she says she wouldn't like to go alone, so maybe I may go with her some day soon if she does not go to Enniskillen again.

I often wonder are you lonely for me and if you *really* miss me, but perhaps you have got used to the separation now. Do you see Mrs McLaverty, Mrs Leigh-Doyle, or any of the ladies I know, or Mrs Duggan? It must be very lonely for you to have no lady, if not.

Paul told me he met you. Larry, with Peggie, called at 44 for the ring,[4] but it was not there. I enclose a cutting from the *Mirror*. Was it Joe H's[5] car that's burned. If so I'm very sorry. I was to have gone to Enniskillen this week-end, but I may go next or week after.

Must finish now. With fondest love.

Your loving
Kit

1. Arthur Griffith, no doubt. His health had begun to decline, and Collins was signalling his return to his office after a spell in a nursing home.
2. Omard was across the county border in the barony of Clonmahon and in the parish of Ballymachugh in Co. Cavan.
3. Commandant Paddy Callaghan who was killed in an ambush laid by the Irregulars at Drumkeen near Collooney, Co. Sligo.
4. 44 Mountjoy Street.
5. Joe Hyland.

Letter 221

Kitty, to Mícheál, Thursday, received 22 July 1922.

My own darling Mícheál,   ·

I remained in bed yesterday until evening, and so I didn't write. I was charmed to-day when I got your letter to know you got back all right.

Overjoyed. I never properly appreciated the meaning of that word before, but that must be how I felt all Tuesday night and Wednesday morning. Overjoyed to see you and know you once more. But it is not at all a pleasant sensation, I mean the *Over*. I mean to say it is not satisfactory. I was electric, I made everything electric! In fact the whole atmosphere was electrical. (Or maybe it was you.)

I was so delighted and surprised that I wanted not to speak at all. Anything I may have said *was* forced. I'd love to have sat just looking at you for hours, but then that was it, I couldn't. I am very simple, I think, in that respect. My real real self would have been to just look at you in wonder.

I am well and happy because I think we love each other even better since last time. Only I'll count the minutes until next time. Hope you had a good sleep last night. I did feel so sorry for you. You were good to write to me yesterday. Fond love and kisses.

Your own
Kit.

Excuse dirty letter written in the Bar!

Letter 222

Mícheál, Portobello Barracks, Dublin, to Kitty, 22 July 1922, telegram.

Am wiring to acknowledge your letter of Thursday. If you get mine of yesterday you may be worrying about Thursday. Fully understand and appreciate. Many thanks and best wishes.

M.

Letter 223

Kitty, to Mícheál, Friday, received 24 July 1922.

My own darling Mícheál,

I sent you a long long letter yesterday, and I hope you got it to-day. I think that letters going up take longer than coming, as I got your letter to-day and also yesterday. I was delighted to get your letter to-day, of course. Glad you didn't think mine too bad, the Tuesday one.

The wire 'am just back' may have meant that, but it read and started with 'Arthur returned tonight' but finished quite un-understandable. I was wondering were you dreaming, or what it meant, and then I thought that you may have thought you told me something of this in a letter.

Well, sweetheart, I suppose you thought that I was in a funny queer mood perhaps when writing yesterday's, but I didn't say half of what I felt. I am no good at describing those sort of feelings and they would be better left unsaid when I can't express myself properly. I realise this when the letter has gone, so it must be the devil for you to try and grasp its meaning; it seems so opposite to my behaviour when I'm with you. However, I do hope that you will understand the spirit of the whole thing, and believe that there was far more in it than may have appeared. So I'll just say no more about it now, only don't think that I'm thinking I've done something wrong in anything like that because, no matter what you say, I'll have those thoughts and feelings. That is my temperament, and it's what always happens when I don't stop to think before I act, or when I live for the moment and forget the future.

It was a great night and just wonderful to see you again. But still I do believe that I am all to blame for certain things. You would have slept and rested but for me, for instance, and that would have done you more good from my point of view, and I'd have been happier in the end (tho' disappointed at first), but to err is human, and I suppose I'm glad I'm that. But I am quite determined that in future I'll try another road and you'll have to help me, and then we'll both reap the reward.

Now I can quite imagine you'll say, 'I'm sorry I went down

at all or saw her for a night. She seems so sorry for it all and that kind of thing'. But you needn't be sorry. You are free from any blame. And you need not imagine I'm sorry, because I'm not. It has taught me one lesson, that it mustn't happen again, no matter how great or noble or generous my love for you.

And, sweetheart, you may think it's all about nothing (and that I've talked more than is necessary) but it means more than nothing to me. However, I'll promise now not to mention it any more in any letter.

How are you, dearest love? I hope you are not still tired after the long runs etc. *I'm* only recovering now. I couldn't believe I'd have felt so tired. A few more strenuous nights like that, and you'd find me dead! I didn't see Paul yet to tell him.

I enclose a speech of L.G.'s.[1] You might like to glance over it if you have time. I just read it in *Sketch* to-day and thought it so cute. You may have seen it, however. If so, there is no harm done, and for *that* matter you mightn't be bothered reading it. I don't know.

Mops is going up to Greystones tomorrow for week-end to G[earóid]. He gets Saturday off. Had you shown any great anxiety for me to go, I'd have accompanied her, just to see Greystones again. And really, dear, if I thought you mightn't have heard it and wouldn't be vexed, I'd have gone sure, and wouldn't tell you because I know how you're situated and could not get off. I must confess I'd love a week-end at any sea place. I'm really considering you in this matter. It would lead perhaps to a misunderstanding if I went without you knowing it, and I'd hate under the present circumstances to even suggest you might be able to come. I'd be satisfied that you were well and safe, and I'd have enjoyed Greystones with Mops. I know it's very cowardly of me not to go with her and tell you afterwards but, when all is said, it might bring too much talk in its train. So good-bye and all my love to you. I pray for you and for us both. Kisses and love and hugs.

Your own
Kit.

1. Lloyd George.

Letter 224

Mícheál, Dublin, to Kitty, 26 July 1922, telegram.

Could not have written yesterday. Did not hear from you
either. Love.

M.

Letter 225

Kitty, to Mícheál, Monday, received 27 July 1922.

My own darling Mícheál,

You will have to excuse this short note. I am writing it
in the shop. I didn't write on Saturday as I missed the post.
I was up in Co. Meath yesterday and had a great day. I'll
tell you about it when I write later. I didn't sleep much last
night and so I'm very tired now and, as Maud is away to-day,
I have to remain in the shop. I think she will be back
to-night. You didn't see her, I suppose? I got no letter to-day.
Hope one comes tomorrow.

How are you? Well, I hope.

Bye bye dear.

Fond love.
Affectionately yours
Kitty.

Letter 226

Kitty to Mícheál, Tuesday, received 27 July 1922.

My very dear Mícheál,

Many thanks for both your letters received to-day. I am
delighted to think you are feeling so fit and well.

Mops isn't back yet. I had a wire from G[earóid] yesterday.
I think she'll be here to-day. Glad you liked my letters and
understand. It is funny, I couldn't write a letter like that
now, but sometimes those things do happen. It would be
tiring to think and write at length always, wouldn't it?

Very glad you can get to Greystones, but an hour is too
short. I was in Nobber on Sunday and saw a good handball
match. I had a few amusing experiences, too, and am glad

I have a sense of humour. Writing this from the shop — I'm
sticking to it well while Mops is away. This evening and for
some days I'll be busy as we are going to the hotel at last.
Larry asked his girl and her sister on a visit from tomorrow,
so I expect I'll be busy fixing up for their arrival. So many
little things to do to make a finish.

Barry, my old boy, was home yesterday. We went over the
old haunts, and he liked the hotel. He says he's praying for
you, but that if you — there is still a chance for *him*! I just
smiled. He'd have called to Greystones to see me only you
might have shot him, but I said you wouldn't be bothered.
I didn't see the papers today. Hope all goes well. I pray
for you.

Bye bye dear.

Fondest love,
Kitty.
X
Just for you.

Hope to see you soon.

Letter 227

Kitty to Mícheál, Wednesday, received 28 July 1922.

My very dear Mícheál,

I wrote you a note on both Monday and Tuesday. I was
sorry to know from your wire this morning that you didn't
hear from me. I didn't write on Saturday and Sunday.
There is no post here.

Mops is back. She said she saw you, and that you looked in
great form. She hasn't gone to Enniskillen yet. I had a letter
from Chrys today asking me to go to Bangor, and I can't
make up my mind. I'd love the sea there and the rest, but I
hate the North. I'll go to Enniskillen for the weekend when
Maud goes there. She enjoyed Greystones. You and I must
have made it fashionable, as all the Dáil seem to have been,
or are, there, including Darrell Figgis and his wife, and
Kevin O'S[1] and his girl who are being married in August.
They are only engaged a short time. They can all afford to
get married, except the chosen Few!

Maud saw Mrs Doyle also who was in great form. She is one of the lucky ones with her unending good time. She had to stay a whole fortnight in Carlow during the trouble and was quite put out. It is funny when you think of it.

I hope things are getting quieter and that you get some rest. I see Gavan Duffy[2] has resigned. Is he a great loss to you?

I must finish for post now, sweetheart. Forgive this uninteresting letter, but I've got no news of interest.

I send you my love and kisses.

Affectionately yours,
Kitty.

1. Kevin R. O'Shiel, a barrister who was active in the land settlement courts of Dáil Éireann during the War of Independence. Subsequently he worked close to Collins and went to London with him occasionally as legal adviser. See L. Ó Broin, *The Prime Informer*, 136.
2. George Gavan Duffy (1882-1951) was a son of the Young Irelander Charles Gavan Duffy. As a solicitor he organised the defence of Roger Casement. He represented South Dublin in Dáil Éireann from 1918 to 1923, was envoy extraordinary in Paris and Rome, and a member of the Irish peace delegation to London. He voted for the Treaty, and was Minister for Foreign Affairs in the Dáil cabinet which, for the time being, continued to exist in parallel with the Provisional Government. His resignation was over the abolition of the republican courts, which he considered a great matter of principle. He explained, however, that he had not disagreed with his colleagues on 'the predominant military question', but he had been uneasy since the start of the Civil War.

Letter 228

Chrys (Mrs Tom Magee), 48 Queen's Parade, Bangor, to Kitty, Monday [possibly 31 July 1922].

My very dear Kitty,

I can't say how glad I was to get your newsy epistle. Tom sent it on from here to Enniskillen. I'm awfully sorry, dear, you have had such an anxious time since, but, thank God, everything is coming right, and the whole people are absolutely with Mick. Kitty, it had to come sooner or later, and the sooner it's over the sooner the country will get

settled down to normal conditions. Every night we offer
up our Rosary and prayers for Mick and Gearóid. May God
bless and protect them.

Won't you come right up here when the baby arrives, and
Tom can act for Mick by proxy at the Baptism. Did you ask
Mick? I don't know where to write to or I would write him.
Then again he is so busy, I hate taking up a minute of his
time with frivolous things. I am keeping splendid considering,
T.G. Bangor is really lovely. It's ideal living here beside
Belfast.

Kitty, do please write me soon again with news of how
you and Mick are. I wish you were married. I think you
would be a thousand times happier and more content. T.G.
you are so well again. Now keep well and don't let anything
worry you. We'll be a long time dead, and the world will
be after us all. I used to think about things, but, T.G., I left
that behind me in Granard. I worried there all my life; now
I suppose I'm almost forgotten, and everything goes on just
as well without me.

No news from Nellie Bly[1] yet, so I wish she had it over.
Her home is beautiful. B. Campbell's baby has not yet
arrived. I gave the girls your message and they always send
you their love. They are all very keen followers of M's at
the Ormeau Road, but I believe Booby, Heber etc. Waterson
and B. Campbell are followers of the Irregulars. Wouldn't
they make you sick, these good-for-nothings? Now with
very fond love to self and Mops, I must end.

Yours always,
Chrys.

[Kitty passed this to Mícheál, adding 'Read the part about
yourself, that's all.']

1. Helen presumably, who was expecting her baby around this time.

Letter 229

Kitty, to Mícheál, Monday, received 2 August 1922.

My own darling Mícheál,

I hope you will forgive me for not writing sooner. When I
was speaking to you on Thursday you asked me if I'd got

your letter *that* day, so when I got back that night I was looking out for one but there was no one. You must have imagined you wrote on Wednesday. You wired all right on Wednesday morning to say you missed the post on Tuesday. I didn't hear from you on Friday but I got your note on Saturday. I also got your letter to-day. I was glad to know you are so well and that you liked my wire. I hope you will be safe when you go South. One can't be too careful, but I'm sure you would smile at this.

We are living in the hotel now. It's not bad. Peggie was here, also her sister[1] who is a lovely artist. First person you have reason to be jealous of. She kept me from writing to you for several days. It was very funny. I was almost jealous of her feet and ankles. Thought they were wonderful altogether. So then we measured both of ours, and we found mine were just as thin as hers, nearly. Wasn't that funny? She plays and sings funny songs for me. We have a piano now.

Writing this in the bar. What a place! The girl is dining (and I'm wining, I.D.T.)[2]. So I'm here. Forgive short note. It's Monday, and it's post time.

Good bye dear.

> Always with love,
> Yours,
> Kate.

1. Angela Sheridan.
2. I don't think.

Harry Boland died on 2 August, following an altercation with the National Army a few days earlier at Skerries, Co. Dublin. Trapped in his hotel, he bolted down a corridor and was shot through the abdomen by a sentry. When Collins heard of his death he came crying into Fionán Lynch's room in 44 Mountjoy Street. There was grievous sorrow here for Kitty also, at a time when her sister Helen was having a baby.

About a week later Collins left Dublin for a tour of inspection in Munster. He was in Tralee on the 12th, at the field headquarters of the South-Western Command, when he learned of Griffith's sudden death. 'There seems to be a malignant fate dogging the fortunes of Ireland,' he told the press, 'for at every critical period in her story the man whom the country trusts is taken from her.' He was thinking of Davis and Parnell, in particular. He declared that he would not retire from his military duties until 'the trouble' was ended (*Irish Independent*, 14 August 1922). He returned to Dublin immediately. Chrys's first child was born the next day, and was named Mícheál. Mícheál and Kitty were his god-parents, and Mícheál sent the child, as a keepsake, a gold ring he had received from the government of China.

Letter 230

Kitty to Mícheál, Tuesday, received 3 August 1922.

My own darling Mícheál,

I got no letter to-day but I know you are very busy. How are you this ages and ages?

I see poor Harry is knocked out. Will I write to him? (Diplomacy.) I wouldn't do so without asking you.

I don't know when I'll go to town as you are so busy just yet, and I wouldn't like to take up your time. However, when I do go, I'll try to be satisfied with an hour or so if you can spare it. I'll be only up for a day or so on account of Bangor.

I'll give Chrys your message. I believe Seán McKeon was home for Sunday night for a few hours for a spree (as they say here) that his mother gave. They seem a very happy pair. She told me at the Show how well you looked in your uniform. She doesn't seem to be a bit nervous about Seán. Well for her that has Athlone and near him, and can see him so often, not like poor me!

The photograph of you in the *Freeman* yesterday was very good, I thought. I must try and get that one later, as I like it. I am still worrying about you. I hope that nothing will happen to you. It is only a fortnight since you came, yet it seems months and months, and do you know that last Sunday one year ago was the day that we first met? G[earóid] wrote to Maud last week asking her what she would like for a present to commemorate it. I had forgotten the exact day

but he remembered. Maud and I were laughing about it.
It certainly was a momentous occasion and we have reason
to remember it. What do you say sweetheart? But I do not
regret it, even tho' you did destroy my peace of mind from
that time! Still I wouldn't exchange with anyone. If only
this thing was over I'd feel quite happy but I'm afraid I might
lose you before I've really had you, no matter what you say.
I had you, in a way, but not sufficient to get tired! (Of
course, I don't mean this, you know.) I send you a big kiss
and a big hug. With all my love.

Your own
Kit.

Letter 231

Mícheál, Dublin, to Kitty, circa 2 August 1922.

My own dearest Kitty,

I was glad to get your letter today. You see you had nearly
forgotten me and were not able to write very cordially on
Monday. It was not possible for me to write to you yesterday,
so I sent a wire this morning and it was before I got your
letter too.

It was no imagining about that letter which you did not
get. I wrote in Merrion St very very early in the morning
before we spoke on the phone — no possible probable
shadow of doubt. It may turn up even yet, but I fear it must
have been captured by the Irregulars.

I mentioned about Harry in yesterday's letter. Last night
I passed Vincent's Hospital and saw a small crowd outside.
My mind went into him lying dead there and I thought
of the times together, and, whatever good there is in any
wish of mine, he certainly had it. Although the gap of
8 or 9 months was not forgotten — of course no one can
ever forget it — I only thought of him with the friendship
of the days of 1918 and 1919. They tell me that the last
thing he said to his sister Kathleen, before he was operated
on, was 'Have they got Mick Collins yet?' I don't believe it
so far as I'm concerned and, if he did say it, there is no
necessity to believe it. I'd send a wreath but I suppose
they'd return it torn up.

Please do come up as soon as you can. You'll excuse
this letter. May God bless you.

Fondest love,
Mícheál.

Letter 232

Kitty, to Mícheál, Wednesday, received 4 August 1922.

My own darling Mícheál,
  I got your welcome letter to-day. My letters evidently
take longer going. I wrote on Monday.
  I hope you will excuse this note. Naturally I feel Harry's
death but I would never have believed that I could feel it
so much. The whole thing's so tragic that to-day I almost
wished I had died too.
  Poor Harry, may he rest in peace. I murmured little
aspirations all day yesterday to Our Lord, to have pity on
the dying. I had an idea he might die, strong and all as he
was. When that hour comes, Oh! vain is the strength of
man. I realise I have lost a good friend in Harry — and no
matter what, I'll always believe in his genuineness, that I
was the one and only. I think you have also lost a friend.
I am sure you are sorry after him. As for Larry, he was
just going up to town to-day to see him. He will motor
up to his funeral, I think, and if I get a seat I'll go for the day
to see you. I hope you are well. When I think of the little
whispering into my ear. *Always* when H. was saying good
bye, he'd say 'don't worry, Kitty, M. will be all right etc'.
He seemed sincere saying that, and it used to make me
happy, and then he'd say, 'Ah I know how to make you
happy'.
  I'll wire you if I go up. It's very undecided yet. You
wouldn't think it right for me to go to his funeral? I sent
a wire to his mother; also I'll send some flowers, tho' they're
not much good to him. He had my rosary beads: I have his.
  Sorry for this note. Good bye dear. Ever yours.

Love,
Kit.

Letter 233

Gearóid Mac Canainn, Government Buildings, Dublin, to Kitty, 4 August 1922, telegram.

Dear Miss Kiernan,
 The Commander-in-Chief told me to ring you up to say he had arranged for lunch at the Shelbourne Hotel, for 1.30 p.m. Room No. 152.

                    Mise, G. Mac Canainn.[1]

1. Originally an employee of the Congested Districts Board. Lost his position through refusing to take the oath of allegiance imposed on civil servants. Worked subsequently in the underground service of the Dáil in various capacities, before becoming Collins's private secretary.

Letter 234

Mícheál, Dublin, to Kitty, 4 August 1922.

My own dearest Kitty,
 I have just cursed the telephone for fifteen minutes. We were cut off just as I had said to you: 'he's always an alarmist.' Then I tried the Hibernian[1] and you were not there. They told me you had gone to Miss Magenni's.[2] Had got as far as this when you came on again. Now the letter is different, but maybe it won't get you until Saturday and then you may have another one before it.
 Anyway I'll go on with it. Now at this moment I'm waiting for you to ring up again. I can't let you know really how glad I was to have seen you this morning and today. It's a long time since I had dinner with you and it was very pleasant.
 You will not misunderstand anything you have heard me say about poor H. You'll also appreciate my feelings about the splendid men we have lost on our side, and the losses they are and the bitterness they cause, and the anguish. There is no one who feels it all more than I do. My condemnation is all for those who would put themselves up as paragons of Irish Nationality, and all the others as being not worthy of concern. May God bless you always.

                    Fondest love, Mícheál.

1. The Royal Hibernian Hotel in Dawson Street.
2. This may have been Kitty's dancing teacher.

Letter 235

Mícheál, Dublin, to Kitty, 8 August 1922.

My own dearest Kitty,
Yesterday I wrote you a note — I think the most hurried
I have ever written to you — most hurried from every point
of view, and God knows today's is not much better. At the
time of writing yesterday I was on the point of setting out
for a long journey, and I did not get back until very late
last night. I was in Maryborough, the Curragh and so on.
It was woefully cold and I was petrified when we arrived
back in Barracks. But I went to bed straight and am feeling
very well this morning.
We have had a hard few days here — the scenes at the Mass
yesterday were really heartbreaking. The poor women
weeping and almost shrieking (some of them) for their dead
sons. Sisters and one wife were there too, and a few small
children.[1] It makes one feel I tell you.
There has been no letter from you. Perhaps you did not
get back on Monday — even if a letter would come at such
speed — which I'm afraid it wouldn't. But you will write,
won't you?
When are you coming up again? You said next week.
And it's next week now. It is you know. And when are
you coming?
Kitty — you won't be cross with me for the way I go
around. I can't help it and if I were to do anything else
it wouldn't be me, and I really couldn't stand it. And
somehow I feel the way I go on is better. And please, please
do not worry.

Fondest love,
Mícheál.

1. The Mass had been celebrated for nine soldiers killed in action in
Kerry.

Letter 236

Kitty, to Mícheál, Tuesday, received 10 August 1922.

My own dear Mícheál,
When you left my room on Saturday, and I felt you had

really gone, I was very lonely. One big tear — but (I proudly answered No)[1] I must hurry up and go home!

We had a lovely run home, at least as far as Nobber. We left about half an hour after seeing you. It was a real summer evening, and quite warm.

Larry and the girls came on here the night before or rather at four in the morning — the car wouldn't go part of the way — and then on Saturday evening Larry met me in Ballyduff[2] and left the girls there. I didn't go to Nobber on Sunday. Went to Gowna instead.

I was delighted to see you again. I got the letter you wrote the day I left here, and the one you must have written while I was in town. Did you think you wouldn't see me again? It was a great surprise to get it.

Maud is in Enniskillen. I don't know when I'll be called to Bangor. I never answered Chrys's letter. Must write to-day.

I may go to town again before I go North, but I am not sure yet. Suppose you are just as busy as ever. I saw you in the paper to-day.

Yesterday was a Bank Holiday. No post going. My mind was very happy leaving town this time — no regrets that way. It was certainly great and I never felt before that I was such pals with you.

Now I must finish with fondest love,

from

Kit.

1. These words, 'I proudly answered No', are from a song, 'For the Green', that was fairly popular at that time at national concerts.
2. Ballyjamesduff in Co. Cavan.

Letter 237

Kitty, to Mícheál, Wednesday, received 11 August 1922.

My own dear Mícheál,

Your letter to-day was just lovely and I was delighted. I got your first note also, on an earlier post.

I'll try not to worry tho' it's hard not to. I am wanting to see you again and am as fond of you as ever. It wouldn't do to get any fonder — because I wouldn't let you go at all then — and then *what* would you do?

I hope to be in town during the Horse Show for about two days. I am to go to Enniskillen this week-end, not sure yet. If I thought you wouldn't be around this way during the week-end, I think I'd go to Enniskillen, but I'm sure you won't be this way.

I didn't get to Confession yet. Hope to soon.

I felt leaving town that we were great friends, and we even hadn't one row. *You* were just great. It would surely have been my fault if _____ and I don't mean a row.

Has Mrs Powell gone? If not, give her my regards.

I am making jam to-day. Awful busy!

You will excuse this, but the time slipped and Larry brought fellows in and left me to talk to them. I eventually left them to write this. I'll write better the next time.

I send you a big hug and millions of kisses.

Your own little pet,
Kit.

Letter 238

Kitty, to Mícheál, received 15 August 1922.

My own dear Mícheál,

In your letter to-day you say 'if I hadn't written there would be letters'. Well, dear, this is not fair as you'll just see. It was too late on Saturday to write — then on Sunday there was no post, and Monday was a holiday here and there was no post either. I wrote on Tuesday and since, but it takes two days to get to Dublin, damn it. I am sorry as I'd love you to get my letters in time.

I was delighted with even your little note, and am longing to see you. Years and years since Saturday.

I'll be in town next week O.K. I'm going to Enniskillen from Saturday to Monday morning. I'll try to speak to you on the phone. Boland of McDonagh and Boland's is here to-day.

I forgot before this to tell you something I heard. Please don't misunderstand my motive. A girl friend told me that a man in Dublin told her that a girl friend of his heard from a society woman — don't know if she's a girl — in London that her only idea in life now is to get spending a night with

Mick Collins. One night will do her, just for the *notoriety* of it.

No wonder the thought of it makes me almost ill. Isn't England rotten? I hope Ireland won't copy England in this respect, at least get so bad. Being a simple Irish girl, I could never get used to that kind of thing, I'm sure, tho' it does seem funny, that London woman's thought of 'notoriety' at your, mine and everybody else's expense. I just thought I'd tell you what I heard.

Now I'll finish sweetheart.

> With all my love,
> Your own
> Kit.

Letter 239

Kitty, to Mícheál, Friday, received 15 August 1922.

My own dear Mícheál,

I am going to Enniskillen this evening. At least I'm going as far as Cavan and getting the first train in the morning to Enniskillen. I'll stay with a girl friend to-night. I'll be in Enniskillen at 11 o'clock to-morrow D.V.

I had a great time with you last night in imagination. It was quite real while it lasted.

First, I'd been making heaps of jam all the evening and was ever so tired. Boland missed his train and I sort of *had* to have him to my new sittingroom with Vi etc. as Larry went away — and Larry had had him for dinner — but I left Boland alone while I made the jam.

Then about 11 o'c when they had all gone I had a nice hot bath and after it I felt so clean and fresh (and looked nice I think) and found myself wishing that *we* could only meet when I'd be after a bath and looking nice. A bit too idealistic and far-fetched perhaps.

Then I went to my room. I was feeling a bit lonely but energetic, so I thought I'd have a bit of a dress rehearsal for you. I just pictured you *there* — as Maud's away. First, I put on a pink and mauve silk pair of pyjamas and asked you how you liked them? Then next a pink pair — and then a nightie. I decided with you that the nightie was the nicest of all, tho' the pyjamas were nice too. Then I gave you a hug and I felt you'd want to hug me etc. All the very loveliest thoughts were in my mind, and then I felt cold and thought how daft I was, and then I got into bed still thinking of you and wishing, wishing for heaps of things.

I can't describe *what* a night I had, almost as good as if you were there. I had the whole top of the house to myself and I could run from mirror to mirror and from room to room.

This morning I had a letter from Mops from Enniskillen. Helen and baby in great form. Boy *of course* a dote, weighed 9 lbs when it was born. She went on to say Helen didn't like 'the whole thing' a bit. *Awful! Awful!* It has put Mops off getting married. Mops says it's not worth it etc. Don't say *I* told you this.

What a sad ending to my dream the night before (a real 'morning after the night before'). A letter like that in the morning left me a wee bit disheartened naturally, and I said the usual thing to myself that perhaps lots say, no marriage for me! Then I thought and thought, would I write you a nice letter etc? I would — I wouldn't — for *several* minutes. Then I remembered you had told me that it can't be all sunshine. I remember this always. Only I do think men are lucky to be men, but I still love you just the same.

Yours in haste,
Kit.

Can you read this letter? There should be several more paragraphs to it which I'm leaving to you. Glad to get your note to-day. I'll be back on Monday. All my love, lovie.

I'll try to dream of you again to-night. It will be hard to better last night's tho'.

Your pet,
K.
Hugs and X.

Letter 240

Kitty, to Mícheál, 14 August 1922.

Have to go to Belfast to-morrow. Was to have gone to town this week. Little M[1] and C[2] in good form. Address 48 Queen's Parade, Bangor. Love.

K.

1. The infant Mícheál.
2. His mother Chrys.

Letter 241

Kitty, to Mícheál, Tuesday, received 17 August 1922.

My own darling Mícheál,

Picture my disappointment. I intended going to town this week, but on Monday morning, when I got back from Enniskillen, there was a wire from Tom to go up to Belfast yesterday. He said 'Chrys and child well'. That's all I know yet. I had hoped it would be at the end of August or later.

I had a nice weekend in Enniskillen, but it was rushed. The baby is a dote, and I took him and he never cried. In fact, he never cried while I was there.

How are you this long, long time? I got your Friday's note yesterday. I didn't write since Friday as I was away. I seem to have lost all my luck. When I think of this time last year, the good time I had during Horse Show week in town. I could see you *every* night, and I not half so fond of you as I am now. Oh, the longing now to see you again and then the awful disappointment. I'd have enjoyed this week in town as Peggie, Angela, Larry, Paddy Cusack and his wife are all there. Larry and his girl are in Dunleary and we arranged to meet, I was so sure I'd be there.

I wired Tom yesterday to say I couldn't go until to-day, I was so tired and nothing ready. Well this morning I got very ill when I was just going off, so had to wire him off again. I'll go to-morrow D.V. It was just disappointment and disgust that made me so ill, I'm sure. I stayed in bed all day and got up for a few hours, so I'm right again. How are you?

Poor Griffith's[1] death is too awful for me to think of,
R.I.P. Was he prepared, I wonder? When that hour comes
what good is anything else? We are just all bits of dust,
the great as well as the small. He will be a loss to you. I can
picture it. How unfortunate it should happen just now.
He was, poor man, evidently overworked, too, and took no
holiday, or at least not in time. I am always thinking of
you and worrying, and just to-night somebody said, that
if you go to the funeral to-morrow you'll be shot, but God
is very good to you, and we must both do Lough Derg[2]
sometime in thanksgiving. Did you ever hear of it? It's very
hard. I did it three times already. I'm sure you will think
this is a sermonising kind of letter.

I'm very lonely to-night and hate to have to go to old
Belfast, yet only I want you and wish to be near you, I'd
love in the ordinary way to be going. Tom's set are more than
nice and I have a few friends there, but I've got a feeling that
I'll be lonely this time and not interested, and then Chrys
won't be in Bangor. But it's not fair to be boring you with
this. I know all you have to contend with, or rather I'd rather
not know *all*.

Perhaps I'll take a run up to town from the North,[3] and
meet Mops there at the end of the week, if Chrys doesn't
mind. Are you lonely for me or too busy and too worried
to think? I send you a kiss with my love.

Yours
Kitty.

I tried to phone you on Sunday but you were not there.
You see, I was thinking of you all the time.

Good bye Mícheál,
Your own loving me.

1. Griffith had been in indifferent health for some time. He had
   entered a nursing home at the instance of his doctors, but insisted
   upon working. He died bending down to tie a boot-lace. The strain
   of the Civil War was too much for him. He was only 51, but twenty
   years older than Collins.
2. A place of penitential pilgrimage near Pettigo, Co. Donegal, on the
   Border with Northern Ireland.
3. 'The run up to town' was to take place in the most tragic circumstances imaginable. Kitty's worst fears were to be realised.

The correspondence ends there. Griffith's funeral took place on 16 August and, after the obsequies, Mícheál and Kitty met, perhaps for the last time. Four days later, he resumed his southern tour. George Bernard Shaw had just made his acquaintance. He was in uniform, apparently, and spoke pleasantly, but 'his nerves were in rags', Shaw said, and he 'kept slapping his revolver all the time he was talking'. Early on the morning of 22 August he left Cork city in a convoy and travelled to Clonakilty and Skibbereen and, as light faded in the late evening, he was on the road back to Cork. At Béal na Bláth near Bandon the party was ambushed and Collins killed. A bullet made a fearful gaping wound at the base of the skull and behind his right ear.

Though Kitty had long acknowledged to herself the danger Mícheál was running and even warned him about it, the news of his death, when it reached her, was completely overwhelming. The bottom just dropped out of her world. Her grief was intense. She became quite hysterical, yet somehow she went up to Dublin, and made her way to the mortuary chapel in St Vincent's Hospital. There the body of Harry Boland had rested three weeks before. Now Mícheál, her Mícheál, lay there, splendid in his uniform with a crucifix on his breast. He might have been Napoleon in marble, Sir John Lavery thought as he started to paint his second picture of him. The chapel was quiet, very very quiet, but the quiet was broken at long intervals by people entering on tiptoe and trying unsuccessfully to control their weeping. Lavery noticed that one woman kissed the dead lips. This, assuredly, was Kitty. On another day she went with Mícheál's sister, the nun, to the City Hall during the lying-in-state and, on the day of the funeral, Maud and she were in the Pro-Cathedral for the Requiem Mass and were given seats on the epistle side near the catafalque. An army despatch rider placed a white flower for her — an Annunciation lily — beside the coffin; and it was, afterwards, the only flower on the gun carriage that bore the body through the crowded streets to Glasnevin.

For weeks she was inconsolable, but her family and close friends gathered round her, and as soon as Maud felt she could do so she took her away to Paris on a holiday. It was

there, with Maud, that she began to contemplate the
uncertain future. That it would be extremely difficult she
knew. Of sympathy for her there would be no stint but she
could not live on sympathy, nor did she want to. If she had
been married to Mícheál the state could have been expected
to look after her. But being just a betrothed was different.
What was she to do then? Where was she to live? These
questions were urgent, with Maud's marriage due to take
place in October, and Larry arranging to bring his bride into
the Greville Arms a few months later. All the Kiernans,
except herself, would then be married. She could hardly go
back to Granard, not to the hotel certainly, or to work
behind the counter in the shop.

She drifted for most of the next year, visiting members of
the family and friends and looking around for an occupation
in the city. She considered various possibilities, even a
career with the Abbey Players, apparently; and was over-
heard declaiming passages from plays in her bedroom. And
when Maud, who had settled in at Dunallen House, the
adjutant-general's residence in Portobello, was expecting a
child, she stayed with her for a while and shared with Seán
Ó Muirthuile the infant's god-parentage. Her general health
was indifferent all the time, however; and the more she
worried the worse it got. Larry was very kind, as he was to
Helen whose married life was disturbed. He encouraged
Kitty to take a break now and again at Greystones in the
Grand Hotel which she had always loved, though it reminded
her now of happy days she had spent there with Mícheál and
'the boys'. She was increasingly introspective, lost some of
her charm, and letter-writing, which she had once found so
easy to do, became virtually impossible for her.

Kitty and Felix Cronin

A change for the better promised for Kitty when she met
another of the handsome young men of the period, Felix
Cronin, who had succeeded Seán Ó Muirthuile as quartermaster-general of the National Army. Felix, who was not
much older than herself, was the eldest of the twelve children
of a national teacher in Lorrha, Co. Tipperary. He had been

through the War of Independence and the Civil War, had met Collins and, like so many of the soldiers of that time, had fallen under his spell. In 1920 he was interned in Wormwood Scrubs but released after a three-week hunger strike. Kitty married him in 1925 and had two children. The first of them was Felix Mary Cronin, the second Michael Collins Cronin, a name eloquent of the affection Felix and Kitty shared for 'the big fellow'.

By then Kitty had recovered her letters to Collins, and retained them with those he had sent her. She always kept them near her so that she could read them over again and again, which she did. She had mislaid some of them, which would explain the many gaps in the correspondence, and she may have destroyed a few of her own letters, which is not altogether unlikely. Felix and she also moved house a number of times which would have increased the risk of loss. She rarely dated her letters, but fortunately Mícheál was so methodical a being that he nearly always indicated on them when he had received them.

Mícheál's letters, were, of course, Kitty's most treasured souvenirs, but almost of equivalent importance in her eyes was the portrait of Collins that Sir John Lavery painted in London, and which she set up on an easel in the principal living room wherever she and Felix resided. That might have led to friction between them for, in the stress of married life, there was always, I would have thought, the risk of unhappy comparisons, that she might occasionally have thought how different things would have been if fate had been kinder to her; but I gather from her sons that the picture gave rise to no such difficulty.

Difficulties arose from other causes, however, principally from the disimprovement in material conditions which followed when Felix, who had held the rank of major-general in the army, went on the reserve of officers in 1929. It was one of those recurring periods of recession: jobs in 'civvy street' were hard to come by, and Felix was perhaps lucky to get an appointment, uncertain though it was, with the Irish Hospitals Trust. This involved him in travelling outside Ireland to promote the sale of sweepstake tickets. The oncoming Second World War ended that particular prospect and he was glad to get a £5 a week job in the Phoenix Park checking turf lorries. His new employers were Fuel Importers Ltd, an organisation set up by the state to cope with one of the problems of the Emergency. It was enormously to Felix's credit, and proof of his unusual ability, that he ultimately became the company's general manager. He also served as a district leader in the local Defence Force.

Money was scarce at times, yet Felix and Kitty managed somehow to send the boys, first, with Maud's son, Gearóid, to Miss Haine's private school on Brighton Square, then to St Mary's, the Holy Ghost College in Rathmines, and, finally, as boarders, to the Dominican College in Newbridge, Co. Kildare. In summertime they could run wild in the countryside round Lorrha, and relax, during the Christmas holidays, in the more genteel life of the Greville Arms in Granard. There they were waited on as 'Master Felix' and 'Master Michael', were fed like fighting-cocks, had their shoes cleaned and their linen washed, had books laid out for them to read, and the piano played for them by Uncle Larry's wife, Peggy. Nothing was too good for Kitty's children.

Kitty and Felix were not so happy, though. They had a problem of incompatibility. They seemed to have difficulty in expressing their affection for each other, in behaving like really close friends. Felix drank excessively at an early stage of the marriage, a habit he had acquired as a result of the indolence of army life after the wars, the social drinking that was part and parcel of his work for Hospitals Trust, and no doubt also in reaction to the shafts from Kitty's sharp tongue, but he recovered completely and became a model husband and father. Kitty was moody, displaying that tendency to create 'misunderstandings and little rows' that Collins had known, and this became so well known to relatives that they went to some trouble to find out what mood she was in before venturing into her company. It was a sad situation that her physical condition may have had something to do with. When she died, according to the medical certificate, it was from commonplace causes, sudden cerebral haemorrhage and hypertension, but endemic in the family was nephritis, the progressive kidney disorder that was once known as Bright's disease. In a space of thirteen years all the Kiernans appear to have died of this: Helen in May 1940, Maud in October 1940, Kitty on 24 July 1945, Larry in December 1948, and Chrys in February 1953. Kitty spent the last three years of her life in and out of nursing homes; the last — the one she died in — was at 36 Elgin Road. They buried her in Glasnevin cemetery, not far from where Collins lies; and Felix joined her there sixteen years later.

Felix and Michael Cronin have preserved the letters ever since, recognising their national importance, and regarding themselves simply as their temporary custodians. They have released them under conditions that ensure their worthy publication before being offered to the National Library of Ireland. After Collins's death Kitty appears to have been reluctant to discuss him with persons outside her family, or to make his letters to her generally available; her sister Helen is named among the acknowledgments in Frank O'Connor's biography of Collins, but Kitty is not. Control over the letters was subsequently very slightly relaxed by her sons to facilitate other biographers of Collins, but it is only now that they can be read in their entirety by anybody.

A View of the Correspondence

The first thing, I think, that should be said about the Collins letters in this collection is that they come to us so unexpectedly. He must have written thousands of letters about the military, party-political and ministerial subjects with which he was concerned, yet one could hardly have anticipated that the first cache to come to light would treat of a love affair, and indeed of one that must be considered unique in the Irish experience.

Immediately noticeable is Collins's handwriting. Despite all the pressures on him, his letters to Kitty are so well formed and legible that it was possible to hand photocopies of them to the typesetter. It is, moreover, surprising that there are so many of his letters in this particular collection. He had entered into an arrangement with Kitty that they should write to each other every other day, and he kept his promise as faithfully as ever he could. He did so even

224

during the tempestuous days of December 1921 when peace
with Britain was being hammered out, and, later, when the
turbulence in the North, the growing opposition to the
Treaty in the South, and his efforts to achieve a 'democratic
constitution' in order to ward off a civil war made his life
little less than a martyrdom. A sequence of letters from
London at the end of May show him near breaking point.
'Things are bad beyond words', he says in one; in another
'Everything is awful. I wish to God someone else was in this
position and not I.' Even Kitty appears to have abandoned
him. 'It's almost heart-breaking', he complains, 'not to have
heard from you; I feel somehow or other that you are not
thinking of me.' Later, when he becomes the Army's
commander-in-chief and she asks him what the role implies,
he does not answer and, of course, there is not a word from
him about the campaign itself. He is obviously suffering. His
last letters to her reveal the painful impact of what is happening in the Civil War. Harry Boland's death, the sight and
sound of women who had lost their sons, the bitterness that
was being generated, affect him deeply. 'There is no one feels
it all more than I do'.

Kitty told Felix Cronin once that in her family she was
regarded as something of a genius at letter-writing. By that
she meant something more than that she could 'dash off'
a letter in time for the post, although, as we can see, she was
very good at doing precisely that, making the editor's job
occasionally more than ordinarily difficult. What she wrote
about was naturally what interested her at the moment,
which was usually herself, the events of the day, and the
course of her affair with Mícheál. She was always promising,
especially when letters tended to peter out with nothing
really said, that she would give him all the news when they
met but, in truth, she had not much to tell him in the way
of news and, not having an interest in politics, she says little
by way of comment on what the newspapers were full of
at the time, the tremendous issues arising from the settlement
with Britain. She read the Irish and English papers and
magazines, of course, but did so primarily to discover what
they were saying, mostly complimentarily, about Mícheál,
and herself. She complains that Mícheál never tells her

much about what is going on: he was deliberately 'most close-mouthed'; but her own lack of political interest or insight, which historians will regret, explains to some extent why Collins, in his letters, was not more forthcoming than he was, not 'rising' even to the suggestion that de Valera disliked him because of his alleged interest in amassing power and had become a rival perhaps, and writing nothing either when she mentions men about whom it would have been instructive to have had a comment from him — Cathal Brugha, Darrell Figgis and George Gavan Duffy. Without mentioning names, the farthest Collins goes is to complain of persons who set themselves up as paragons of nationalism and virtue.

Kitty never ceases to express concern about the life of strain Mícheál is being forced to lead, a life of endless meetings and interviews. She presses him to try and get some sleep, but this is usually impossible. Indeed he seems to be trying at times almost to do without sleep altogether, to be content to snatch a few hours late at night in Greystones. In Granard he sometimes falls asleep, leaving Kitty to do without his company, much though she yearns for it. They both sigh for a normal life in marriage and get as far as looking for a house, but normality is not on the horizon, and Mícheál finds it impossible to conform to any plans that are made for a wedding. Indeed it seems that the day on which he died was one of a number that had been designated for that purpose.

Kitty had ideas of domestic bliss that would have amused Mícheál, as they do us, but I am sure he understood what she was getting at. She wanted the normality she had seen her parents enjoy, and sensed the dangers confronting Mícheál that stood in the way of its achievement. He was, in fact, caught in a vice.

Kitty's letters are occasionally more than just well written. That, for instance, in which she describes a persistent local suitor she has rejected; or the letter in which she tells Mícheál of her meeting with the West Cork commando Tom Barry; or those in which she opens her heart to him with unusual frankness.

Collins's letters, as love letters, are more discreet, more subdued, than Kitty's — that might be expected of a man whose intelligence work during the fight with Britain was so highly acclaimed — but they do not conceal his affection for her, his concern for her health, his eager anticipation of her becoming his wife. He was a lover of children — that we know from other sources — and would have loved to have had a family of his own.

A feature of the correspondence is its recurrent religious note. Both Mícheál and Kitty had an abiding sense of the spiritual, as indeed had Harry Boland. In her first letter Kitty hopes that Mícheál will say a prayer for her; in her last she suggests they 'do' Lough Derg together, which would have meant going barefoot for three black-fast days, and a dreary night vigil. Mícheál would have faced up to the ordeal, I feel sure. He practised his faith in the honest-to-God way that was common not so long ago, and which did not prevent him from using coarse expletives in moments of exasperation. An appendix to Beaslai's two-volume biography shows him startling a Passionist missioner by arriving extra early on the morning of his departure to the London peace talks to make a general confession — I have put in the National Library a letter from the missioner confirming this story — and in London going to Mass daily in order to obtain spiritual support for the burden he had been called upon to carry. He lit candles for Kitty, as she had taught him to do, and gave the details to her. That may seem sanctimonious or pietistic, but to think so would be to misunderstand altogether the nature of a relationship in which it was possible for a man and woman to talk sincerely to each other about their religious beliefs and what lay behind them, about their rosaries and the cult of the Little Flower. It was not at all strange in that context for Kitty to wonder whether Arthur Griffith had been ready to meet his Maker, and she would have hoped and prayed that Collins, when his time came, was likewise prepared. I like to put that reflection, and the discretion with women that can be read into Collins's letters, against the allegations of his womanising that were circulated at the time of the Civil War and that, regretfully, are still retailed today. Interestingly, there is no trace of bitterness in his letters for the men and women who had become his enemies and detractors and no questioning of their moral condition.

227

Select Bibliography

Beaslaí, Piaras, *Michael Collins and the Making of a New Ireland*, 2 vols, Dublin 1926
Cronin, Seán, *The McGarrity Papers*, Tralee 1972
Dáil Éireann, *Official Reports*
Dwyer, T. Ryle, *Michael Collins and the Treaty*, Dublin and Cork, 1981
———, *De Valera's Finest Hour*, Dublin and Cork, 1982
Forester, Margery, *Michael Collins, The Lost Leader*, London 1971
Gaughan, J. Anthony, *Austin Stack*, Dublin 1977
Griffith, Kenneth and O'Grady, Timothy E., *Curious Journey*, London 1982
Jones, Thomas, *Whitehall Diary: III, Ireland 1919-25*, ed. K. Middlemas, London 1971
Lavery, John, *Life of a Painter*, London 1939
Longford, Earl of, and O'Neill, Thomas, *Eamon de Valera*, Dublin 1970
Lyons, F. S. L., *Ireland Since the Famine*, London 1971
Macardle, Dorothy, *The Irish Republic*, Dublin 1937
MacEoin, Seán, 'Unpublished autobiography'
McKenna, Kathleen Napoli, 'In London with the Treaty Delegation: personal recollections', *Capuchin Annual* 1971
Moynihan, Maurice, *Speeches and Statements by Eamon de Valera*, Dublin 1980
Neeson, Eoin, *The Civil War in Ireland, 1922-1923*, Cork 1966
Ó Broin, León, *Michael Collins*, Dublin 1980
O'Connor, Frank, *The Big Fellow*, Dublin 1965
Ó Luing, Seán, *Art Ó Gríofa*, Dublin 1953
Ó Muirthuile, Seán, *Memoir* (Mulcahy Papers, UCD Archives)
Pakenham, Frank, *Peace by Ordeal*, London 1935
Taylor, Rex, *Michael Collins*, London 1958
Younger, Calton, *Ireland's Civil War*, London 1968

229

Index